EMPATH

A Complete Guide for Developing Your
Gift and Finding Your Sense of Self

BY JUDY DYER

EMPATH: A Complete Guide for Developing Your Gift
and Finding Your Sense of Self
by Judy Dyer

ISBN: 978-1989588130

ALSO BY JUDY DYER

The Empowered Empath: A Simple Guide on Setting Boundaries, Controlling Your Emotions, and Making Life Easier

The Highly Sensitive: How to Stop Emotional Overload, Relieve Anxiety, and Eliminate Negative Energy

Narcissist: A Complete Guide for Dealing with Narcissism and Creating the Life You Want

Anger Management: How to Take Control of Your Emotions and Find Joy in Life

Borderline Personality Disorder: A Complete BPD Guide for Managing Your Emotions and Improving Your Relationships

Empaths and Narcissists: 2 in 1 Bundle

To my mother, Linda
for your patience, love, kindness, humor,
and willingness to help others.

CONTENTS

PART 1 .... **9**

Introduction 11

Your Free Gift 13

Chapter 1: What is an Empath? 17

Chapter 2: How to Embrace Your Gift 31

Chapter 3: Understanding Energy 35

Chapter 4: Empaths and Spiritual Hypersensitivity 43

Chapter 5: Empaths, Insomnia, Exhaustion,
            and Adrenal Fatigue 56

Chapter 6: How to Protect Yourself from Energy
            Vampires 66

Chapter 7: Empaths and Work 71

Chapter 8: Normalizing and Maintaining Your Gift 79

Chapter 9: How to Support a Young Empath 84

Conclusion 93

PART 2 ....**95**

Introduction 97

Chapter 10: How to Develop Your Chakras 98

Chapter 11: How to Manage Your Negative
             Emotions 106

Chapter 12: How to Deal With Anxiety 112

Chapter 13: How to Control Your Energy 130

Chapter 14: The Most Effective Grounding
            Techniques 141

Chapter 15: How to Turn Your Empath Gift Into
            a Superpower 158

Conclusion 177

Essential Oil Recipes for Anxiety 183

PART 1

INTRODUCTION

Greetings readers! Congratulations on taking the first step on your journey to greatness as you begin to understand and use your gift for the greater good! If you are reading this, I can only assume that you have just become conscious of your gift as an empath and are new to the subject. You are probably both scared and excited; scared because you don't quite understand it and excited because you are about to step into a new realm of possibilities that you had no idea existed.

Empaths who are not in control of their gift find it a terrible source of stress, pain, and anxiety. Feeling other people's emotions as though they are your own can feel as if you are on a constant emotional roller coaster. The purpose of this book is to bring you to a place of rest concerning the gift you have been endowed with. You will learn exactly what your gift is and why you are so privileged to have it.

I want you to understand that you are carrying great power, and the reason it affects you in such a profound way is due to the dynamism of it. There are many benefits and blessings associated with being an empath, and as you learn to embrace your gift, doors of opportunity will begin to open for you.

Take your time to fully understand and absorb each chapter before moving on to the next. Prepare your spirit for the keys you are going to find in this book that will unlock the abundance of potential within you.

To maximize the value you receive from this book, I highly encourage you to join our tight-knit community on Facebook. Here you will be able to connect and share with other like-minded empaths to continue your growth.

Taking this journey alone is not recommended, so this can be an excellent support network for you.

It would be great to connect with you there,

Judy Dyer

To Join, Visit:

www.pristinepublish.com/empathgroup

YOUR FREE GIFT

As a way of saying thanks for downloading this book, I'm offering the book *Hygge: Discovering the Danish Art of Happiness* FREE to my readers. It was written by a close friend of mine named Olivia Telford, who has kindly allowed me to share it with you.

With *Hygge*, you'll discover something that offers relaxation, happiness, and contentment, all rolled into one. It is a way of being and living that has been adopted by countless numbers of people throughout Scandinavia and the wider world. It reflects a "coziness" that encompasses the positivity and enjoyment one can get from simple, everyday things.

Visit: www.pristinepublish.com/hygge

DOWNLOAD THE AUDIO VERSION OF THIS BOOK FREE

If you love listening to audiobooks on-the-go or would en-joy a narration as you read along, I have great news for you. You can download the audiobook version of *Empath* for FREE just by signing up for a FREE 30-day Audible trial!

Visit: www.pristinepublish.com/audiobooks

CHAPTER 1:

WHAT IS AN EMPATH?

An empath is a person with an open spirit; they unconsciously sense things in the unseen and the seen realms to the point where it can become a burden. They pick up on the energy surrounding them and have a natural ability to tune in to the feelings of others. They are influenced by other people's moods, thoughts, desires, and wishes. Being an empath is not limited to high

sensitivity and emotions; they intuitively know the intentions and motivations of others. Being an empath is not something that is learned; you are either born this way or you're not. As an empath, you are constantly in touch with the feelings and energy of others, which means you are continuously bearing the weight of the emotions of those around you.

Many empaths are prone to the physical manifestations of the emotions they are burdened with, such as daily aches and pains and chronic tiredness. I am sure you have heard the saying, "You look like you're carrying the weight of the world on your shoulders!" This is exactly what empaths do! They carry the energy, emotions, and karma of everyone they come in contact with.

Empaths are extremely humble; they shy away from compliments and would rather give praise to someone else than receive it. They express themselves with great passion and talk very candidly, which can sometimes cause offense. They are not the type of people who hide their feelings; they will open up to anyone who cares to listen.

On the flip side, they can be very anti-social and will gladly block out of their lives those who they feel are hindering them in some way. They may not realize they are doing this; to the empath who doesn't understand who they are, this is often their way of shutting out the feelings and energy from others that they constantly have to deal with.

Although empaths are sensitive to the emotions of others, they don't spend much time listening to their own heart. This can lead them to put the needs of others before their own. An empath is typically non-aggressive, non-violent, and quick to become the peacemaker between people. An empath feels extremely uncomfortable in an environment of disharmony; they avoid confrontation and quickly make amends if a situation gets out of hand. If they lose control and say something that offends, they resent themselves for it and will make a swift apology.

Empaths tend to pick up the feelings of others and then project them back to the person without realizing what they are doing. When an empath is in the beginning stages of understanding their gift, it is advised that they talk things out in order to release the buildup of emotions. If not, they tend to bottle things up and build skyscraper walls around themselves and refuse to let anyone in. This inability to express their feelings is often the result of a traumatic event, a childhood in which emotions were not expressed in the home, or parents who believed that children are "to be seen and not heard."

Emotional withdrawal can have a negative effect on physical health; the longer we hold our emotions inside without release, the more power they have over us. When emotions build up, there will eventually be a release and that release is never a good thing. Humans are wired to express themselves when they feel a burden; it is how healing takes place. When you talk something out, there is an emotional relief that comes from no longer carrying the weight alone. If this doesn't take place, there is a risk of mental and emotional instability as well as negative emotions manifesting in the form of an illness.

Empaths have sensitivity towards movies, TV, videos, and news broadcasts that depict scenes of violence or physical or emotional pain and trauma, whether it involves an adult, child, or animal. This can reduce them to tears and cause them to become physically ill. They are unable to justify the suffering that they feel and see and have no tolerance for those who don't share the same level of compassion.

Empaths typically work in careers that enable them to help others, whether it's with animals, nature, or people. They are passionate about their work and their dedication to others. You will often find empaths in volunteer positions, dedicating their time to helping others without pay or recognition.

Due to their ceaseless imagination, empaths are great storytellers; they are constantly learning and asking questions. They are also very gentle and romantic; they have a passion for family history and will keep old photos, jewelry, or other items of value that have been passed down through the generations. They are often the ones who sit and listen to stories told by grandparents and great-grandparents and hold a wealth of knowledge about the history of their family.

To suit the variety of moods that they experience, they listen to a range of music genres. People are often curious about their taste in music, especially the diversity of it. One minute they are listening to classical music and the next hardcore rap! The lyrics of a song can have a powerful effect on an empath, especially if it relates to something they have recently experienced. It is advised that empaths listen to music without lyrics to avoid sending their emotions into a spin.

Empaths use body language as a form of expression; they can articulate themselves just as easily through dance, body movements, and acting as they can through words. Empaths are capable of exhibiting high amounts of energy when they dance; they get lost in the music and enter into a trance-like state as their spirits sync with the beat and the lyrics. They describe this feeling as becoming completely lost in the moment; they are no longer aware of the presence of others.

Empaths have very attractive spirits, and people are naturally drawn to them without understanding why. They will find that complete strangers feel comfortable talking to them about the most intimate subjects and experiences. Another reason why empaths are so magnetic is that they are very good listeners; they are bubbly, outgoing, enthusiastic and people love to be in their presence. They are often the life and soul of a party, and people like to have them around because they feed off their energy. Due to the extreme nature of their personality, the opposite can also be true; their moods can switch in an instant and people will scatter like cockroaches to get away from them. If an empath doesn't understand their gift, the burden of carrying so many emotions can be overwhelming. They don't understand that they are feeling someone else's emotions; it is confusing to them. One moment they are fine and the next they are feeling a tsunami of depression, which causes them to act out.

It is not a good idea to abandon an empath at the height of one of their mood swings. Whoever is around at this time should lend them a shoulder to cry on, become compassionate, and be a listening ear. This return of empathic emotional care will often lead to an instant recovery. Empaths are often misunderstood, and it is a crucial part of their journey that not only do they understand themselves but others around them do too.

Empaths are often thinkers and problem solvers; they love to study a variety of different materials. They believe that problems and solutions exist together and that there is always a solution at hand. They will often search until they find the answer to a problem, which can be a great benefit to others around them, whether at work or home. The empath is often capable of tapping into the knowledge of the universe and receiving the guidance they need to solve the problem they have put their minds to.

Empaths are dreamers; they have vivid and detailed dreams. They believe their dreams are linked to their physical reality and that they are being warned about something that is happening in their life or the life of someone they know. From a young age, they invest their time and effort into unlocking the mysteries of their dreams.

Empaths thrive off mental engagement; they have no desire for the mundane and find it difficult to focus on things that don't stimulate them. When they find themselves getting bored, they will often resort to daydreaming and will settle into a detached state of mind. Although their physical body is in the same location, their mind is in another dimension.

A teacher will hold the attention of an empath student only if he or she is as expressive and emotional as that student is; if not, the student will quickly switch off. Similarly, if empaths do not completely captivate their audience, they lose interest. They make the best actors because of their innate ability to become so subjugated by the feelings of others that when they play a role, the emotions of their character completely take the place of their own.

They are prone to experiencing synchronicities and déjà vu. What begins as a set of continuous coincidences leads to an understanding that seeing into the future is a part of who the empath is. As this acceptance becomes a reality, a feeling of euphoria sets in as they begin to connect with the power of their gift.

Many empaths have a deep connection to the paranormal; they will have a number of near-death and out-of-body experiences throughout their lives. Traveling in the spirit realm to another dimension is a normal occurrence in the life of an empath. They are free spirits and the mundane routine of life is not what they live for. When they get stuck in a rut or cycle, all meaning of life is lost and they are forced to stop, re-examine their life, and get back on the journey of self-discovery. Their paranormal experiences lead to isolation; to the average person this is not the norm and so the empath tends to suppress their abilities in fear of being labeled negatively. However, they are capable of overcoming this fear and that typically arises when they are surrounded by other empaths.

THERE ARE A VARIETY OF DIFFERENT TYPES OF EMPATHS AND EACH USES A DIFFERENT PSYCHIC EMPATHIC TRAIT. THEY ARE AS FOLLOWS:

1. **Geomancy:** Geomancers have the ability to feel Earth's energy; when they are on certain land and in certain places, they can feel the energy. When a natural disaster is about to take place, regardless of where it is happening, they get headaches.

2. **Telepathy:** These empaths have the ability to read the thoughts of others.

3. **Psychometry:** These have the ability to receive energy from impressions, places, photographs, or objects.

4. **Physical healing:** The ability to feel the physical symptoms of others in their own body, which they can then use to promote healing.

5. **Animal communication:** The ability to feel, hear, and communicate with animals.

6. **Emotional healing:** The ability to feel the emotions of others.

7. **Nature:** The ability to communicate with nature and plants.

8. **Mediumship:** The ability to feel the energy and the presence of spirits.

9. **Knowing or claircognizance:** The ability to know what has to be done in any given situation;

this is often coupled with a feeling of calm and peace in the midst of a crisis.

10. **Precognition:** The ability to feel when something significant is about to take place. This is often an unexplainable feeling of doom or dread.

IF YOU ARE UNSURE ABOUT WHETHER OR NOT YOU HAVE THE GIFT OF AN EMPATH, HERE ARE 25 COMMON EMPATH TRAITS:

1. They look for the victim, the underdog; those going through emotional trauma and suffering draw the attention of the empath.

2. The empath is highly creative with a vivid imagination; they are usually multitalented with the ability to sing, dance, draw, act or write. An untidy environment full of chaos and mess blocks the flow of energy for the empath; they are very minimalist and tidy.

3. They have a disdain for narcissism. Although empaths are very tolerant, compassionate, and kind, they don't like to be around egotistical characters who live for themselves and have no consideration for the feelings and emotions of others.

4. They sense energy in food. Empaths are often vegetarian because they can feel the suffering that the animal experienced while being slaughtered.

5. They don't like buying second-hand goods, as they believe that anything previously owned by someone else carries their energy. When the empath is financially stable, they prefer to buy a brand new house or car so they are not stepping into someone else's energy.

6. They spend time daydreaming. An empath can get lost in their imagination; they can happily stare into oblivion for hours. If an empath is not being stimulated, they get bored and distracted. Whether they are at home, work, or school, they must be interested in what they are doing or they will drift.

7. They are knowledge seekers. Empaths are always learning something new; they find it frustrating when they have unanswered questions, and they will go above and beyond the call of duty to find the answer. If they feel a nudge in their spirit that they have an answer, they will look for confirmation. The negative side of this is that they carry too much information, which can be draining. They have a deep desire to know more about the world.

8. They can't participate in what they don't enjoy. They feel as if they are not being truthful to themselves when they engage in activities that they don't like. Many empaths are labeled as lazy because they refuse to take part in anything they don't agree with, and that happens to be the majority of things.

9. They have a need for isolation. They must get time alone, which is even true of empath children.

10. They have a love of animals and nature. Empaths enjoy life outdoors and being at one with nature. They typically have pets inside the home. They believe that plants and animals have feelings and emotions.

11. They are very much in touch with the supernatural realm and things like seeing ghosts and spirits are normal to them. They also seem to have access to information that scientists spend years trying to attain. For example, empaths knew the world was round when everyone else believed it was flat.

12. They are always tired; because they are so exposed to other people's energy, they constantly feel drained and tired. This tiredness is so extreme that even sleep can't relieve it. Empaths are often diagnosed with Myalgic Encephalomyelitis (ME). They suffer from back problems and digestive disorders. The center of the abdomen is where the solar plexus chakra is located (see chapter 10). Empaths feel the emotions of others in this area, which weakens it and can lead to irritable bowel syndrome, stomach ulcers, and lower back problems. The empath who doesn't understand their gift will typically suffer from such physical problems. They catch illnesses quickly; an empath develops the physical symptoms of those around

them. They often catch the flu, eye infections, and aches and pains in the body and joints. When they are close to someone who is unwell, they often experience sympathy pains.

13. The empath is a sounding board. Everyone goes to the empath to unload their problems, which often end up as their own. They feel and take on others' emotions. They can feel the emotions of those close by, far away, or both. The more experienced empath knows when someone is thinking badly of them.

14. They can detect lies. When someone is not telling the truth, the empath is aware, and when someone is thinking or feeling one way but saying something else, they know. They don't need to listen to the tone of someone's voice or analyze their facial expressions to know they are lying; they have the ability to know instantly whether or not someone is telling the truth.

15. They find it difficult to watch any type of violence, nor can they read about it in newspapers and magazines. As a result of this, empaths find it difficult to watch TV or read newspapers and magazines.

16. They are often overwhelmed in public places. Being in places like supermarkets, stadiums, and shopping malls where there are a lot of people is difficult for the empath because of the amount of energy that is being released from the crowds. Their envi-

ronment is arranged and managed to work around their sensitivities. Their schedule and commitments are arranged to avoid chaotic, unpleasant situations that are overly stimulating.

17. They have access to advanced knowledge. Empaths are tuned into knowledge; they know things without being told. This is not merely a gut feeling or intuition; their knowledge comes from a greater source of power. The more they are tuned into their gift, the stronger this gift becomes.

18. They are capable of influencing the moods of others. They are very charismatic, and people are attracted to their energy. When they spend too much time around people, they start to speak and act like them.

19. They like to be around water; they enjoy the energy from oceans, rivers, and seas.

20. They have always been told that they are too emotional and sensitive. Their ability to pick up on feelings and cues is not normal to everyone else, but it is to them.

21. They have a low tolerance for pain; they find it difficult to get injections and feel ill when they have to deal with even the smallest of injuries. Doctors may even tell them they complain too much.

22. They are very observant and extremely good at reading facial expressions and body language.

23. They are drawn to healing professions; empaths are often nurses, doctors, or veterinarians. Empaths are drawn to becoming counselors, social workers, psychologists, animal communicators, teachers, and caretakers.

24. Empaths are drawn to alternative and spiritual arts such as organic nutrition, hypnotherapy, psychotherapy, holistic medicine, energy and Reiki practices, and psychic reading. They have an interest in metaphysical activities such as prayer, meditation, yoga, and positive affirmations.

25. They are non-conformists and choose to live outside of the constraints of society's norm of a job, a family and 2.4 children. They enjoy traveling, adventure, and freedom. Empaths are free spirits; they don't like to remain stagnant. They don't like rules, routine, or control. An empath likes to have the freedom to do what they want to do when they want to do it. If they are unable to do so, they feel restricted and imprisoned.

CHAPTER 2:

HOW TO EMBRACE YOUR GIFT

As you have read, being an empath is physically and emotionally exhausting, which can cause you to feel as if you don't have a gift but a burden. Feeling this burden is the first step towards embracing your gift. You now need to learn how to look after yourself so you can embrace your gift without feeling exhausted. This is an extremely important process, and you should invest time and effort into mastering the most effective coping mechanisms. Once you learn how to cope and function as an empath, you can use your gift to better yourself and your environment.

Due to the constant overwhelming emotions and stress, you must go to great lengths to eliminate the negative energy you can attract. The techniques that you learn should become a part of your daily routine and will open your eyes to the true value of the gift you have been blessed with.

Even though being an empath is not a disease or a curse, it is controversial and can cause you to feel so uncomfortable that you may try to suppress it. In Alcoholics and Narcotics Anonymous the slogan is: "the first step to a cure is to admit that you have a problem." The same applies to you as an empath; the first step towards embracing your gift is admitting that you are indeed an empath and that you are proud of it. Although this is a small step, it will make a great difference, as you will eliminate a lot of the stress associated with hiding your gift.

To feel relieved from the struggles of being an empath, you must get enough rest. The most effective method of doing so is to set a regular sleep-wake cycle and do what you can to ensure you have a restful sleep throughout the night (see chapter 5). You should also take regular breaks throughout the day for relaxation and deep breathing exercises to rid yourself of some of the stress that has built up throughout the day. Such exercises will provide you with immediate relief (see chapter 7).

Take care not to place yourself in environments that are overly stimulating on a regular basis. It can be difficult to avoid them completely, however, you should endeavor to avoid them as much as you can. If you know you are going to be in an overly-stimulating environment, make sure that you prepare yourself emotionally and mentally beforehand. This will enable you to quickly rid yourself of the stress you feel as a result of the energy you are surrounded by.

Social media and the internet in general are extremely stimulating environments. It is advised that you often take a break from the energy that is emitted through the internet. You don't have to be in the physical presence of someone to absorb their energy.

It is also advised that you have a regular routine in place for stress relief. What you do depends on what you find relaxing. You might enjoy reading motivational books, getting a massage, going to a spa, using aromatherapy, or taking a warm bath.

HERE ARE SOME HELPFUL TIPS TO ASSIST YOU IN FULLY EMBRACING YOUR GIFT:

APPRECIATE AND HONOR YOUR STATE OF CONSCIOUSNESS

Empaths often feel pressure because they are different. Being different brings many challenges because the world expects you to conform to its norms and values. When you are misunderstood by others, it is easy to take their disapproval personally and carry it as a burden. It is normal to be empathic and a gift to be in tune with yourself physically and spiritually. I would go as far as saying that it is essential that you have this gift to survive because it puts you on high alert when danger is surrounding you or your family.

IDENTIFY THE DIFFERENCE BETWEEN THOUGHT CONSCIOUSNESS AND EMPATHIC CONSCIOUSNESS

You can observe the difference between day and night because you can see it. It is difficult to identify empathic awareness because you can't see it. It is something that is felt and experienced on the inside. Once you can identify this difference, you will begin to see your gift as a blessing instead of a curse. You attain self-knowledge when you know when the mind and its thoughts are dominating. Feelings and thoughts are different, and when you recognize these differences, you will feel liberated. This knowledge will give you the power to defend yourself against energetic tides instead of being pulled into them.

TRUST YOUR INTUITION

The majority of empaths awakening to their gifts ignore their gut instincts. Don't do this; your intuition is always correct. This does not mean that you should fully understand or embrace the feeling. You may not have complete knowledge of the situation, but the feeling is real, and you should embrace the deeper communication that is happening within.

CHAPTER 3:

UNDERSTANDING ENERGY

O nce an empath starts to embrace their gift and understand that they don't have to carry other people's
energy around with them, a natural curiosity about
energy sets in. Through your symptoms and experiences,
you become aware of how powerfully energy can affect you
in a negative way. If this is the case, it is also possible that
energy can have a positive effect on you. Once you have
learned how to deal with the stress of carrying energy, it
then frees you to learn how you can use energy positively.
Learning how energy works is an exciting adventure, and it

can take you to places in life that you didn't think existed. As you have read, many empaths become healers; these are the people who have learned how to embrace their gift because they understand how their energy can have a positive effect on others.

The first step in learning about energy is to understand how to ground yourself from different energy. This will help you to avoid becoming overwhelmed by the energy you can feel. One of the most popular grounding techniques is visualization. This is a method by which you consciously imagine yourself being grounded. Here are some steps to get you started:

Sit comfortably in a chair and position both feet firmly on the ground with your palms facing upwards. Don't force yourself into a certain position; simply allow your body to relax into the chair. Imagine that a piercing white light is radiating from the sun and through your crown chakra, leaving the bottom of your spine and then moving into the earth's center. Imagine that, as your body is being filled with the white light, negative black energy is being released through your palms. When your entire body has been filled with the white light you will naturally relax knowing that you are now filled with positive and peaceful energy.

Practice visualization on a regular basis to keep you grounded to the earth underneath you, to release the negative energy that has attached itself to you, and to enhance your empath gift.

Working confidently with energy will stop you feeling as if you are out of control. It will enable you to protect and heal yourself and the people who are placed in your path. Ultimately, it will give you the ability to control the energy that is directly affecting you.

There are many things you can excel in when you learn to handle energy effectively; this is one of the reasons the ability to do so is so attractive to many. It is your divine right to learn how to navigate this powerful terrain so you can use energy in a way that benefits you and others.

MEDIUMISTIC ABILITIES

A medium uses their intuitive or psychic abilities to see into the past, present, and future of an individual's life by tuning into the spirit energy surrounding that person. Mediums are reliant on the presence of a spiritual energy outside of themselves to gain accurate information about the person they are reading. In the work of mediumship, a connection is made with the dead to deliver messages to those who are alive. Information is received directly from the dead, angels, and spirit guides. There are four main types of mediumship:

CLAIRSENTIENCE

You strongly sense the emotions and feelings of people, spirits, animals, and places. You feel these emotions both in your heart and in your body; you also feel the presence of spirits. If you have clairsentient abilities:

- You are very sensitive to your surroundings; you easily sense the vibe of a person or place.

- You have unexplainable physical or emotional reactions when you go to places where there are large crowds.
- Your emotions change suddenly when you are around people or when you arrive at a person's home.
- You know what people are feeling without them telling you; you can empathize with people easily.
- You can feel the presence of spirits.
- When people are in pain, you can feel it in your own body.
- You use the words "I feel" when you are having conversations with others.
- You can taste and smell things from the spirit world.

CLAIRCOGNIZANCE

Information comes to you spontaneously; you don't doubt it and you believe in your soul that it is 100 percent accurate. This information will either come in the form of figures and facts, or you just know the truth of a situation, a person, or a career path. If you have claircognizant abilities:

- You receive the answers to things and don't understand how or where they came from.
- You have very inspirational, creative, and beneficial ideas.
- Your mind is never still; you are always coming up with a new idea, especially when you are working on a project.

- You automatically know when someone is telling the truth.
- You tend to use the words "I know" when having conversations with others.

CLAIRVOYANCE

You see things as images in your mind or as a precognition in dreams before they manifest. If you have clairvoyant abilities:

- You constantly have very vivid dreams.
- You are very imaginative and spend a lot of time daydreaming.
- You always speak in metaphors.
- You can see shapes, colors, pictures, or objects when you close your eyes to sleep or during meditation.
- You see flashes of light, sparkly lights, or movements out of the corners of your eyes.
- You often use the words "I see" when you are talking to others.

CLAIRAUDIENCE

You hear messages either inside your mind or audibly. For the majority of people, these messages come in the form of telepathic communication, meaning that the spirits will have a conversation with you through your thoughts. You can have a conversation with the spirits and they will reply. If you have clairaudient traits:

- You listen more than you talk.

- You speak to plants and animals because you believe they can communicate with you.
- You often feel as if you are the recipient of telepathic information.
- When you provide really helpful advice, you quickly forget what you said and wonder where you got such wise information.
- You often hear buzzing or ringing in your ears. You experience the same sensation in your ears as you do just before they pop on an airplane.
- You use the words "I hear you" when speaking to people.

Due to the intuitive nature of empaths, they are often drawn to mediumistic abilities. This is not a natural trait of an empath, but that doesn't mean you can't have the gift; it is easier for an empath to develop this gift because of their sensitivity to the spirit world. If you feel you are being drawn to this space and you decide you want to develop this skill, you should not take it lightly and it's crucial that you find a good teacher. As you have now learned, empaths absorb all types of energy, whether positive or negative, and if you get in contact with the wrong spirit, it will torment you.

PSYCHIC ABILITIES

Empaths are capable of sensing things before they manifest; psychic ability is strongly connected to your ability to "just know." You will often have visions or premonitions about things before they happen. You can't learn how to have visions or premonitions, but you can train yourself to have them whenever you need to. This provides you with the wonderful and powerful ability to be able to predict future events. You may not have experienced any premonitions or visions yet, but this doesn't mean you can't operate with that gift; it may be that you just haven't tapped into it yet. As you learn how to control this gift, you will find it easy and exciting to predict the future.

ENERGY PROJECTION

One of the things you may not be aware of as an empath is that you can send energy to people. When you do so you are giving that individual the particular sensation or vibe you want them to experience. This is a skill used for remote healing, in which empaths are capable of healing people when they are not even in their presence. Others use this as a way of praying for people and sending good energy and thoughts in the direction of another person to help them to get through a difficult time when they are unable to be there personally. Sending energy is not limited to empaths; everyone can do this if they put their mind to it. However, when empaths send energy, the recipient is more likely to feel it because they have a powerful connection to the energy source.

Healing

Empaths understand the connection between energy and people. This is referred to as an energy body, and it can become inflicted with illness or pain. When you are trained in energy healing, you learn how to work with your own or another person's energy body to induce healing.

CHAPTER 4:

EMPATHS AND SPIRITUAL HYPERSENSITIVITY

Empaths often suffer from spiritually based hypersensitivity; the symptoms include:

- Your environment causes you to feel overwhelmed
- Sounds are too loud, even if made at a normal range
- You constantly feel the feelings of others

This type of energetic overwhelm is nothing new; the spiritual community has been dealing with it for many years. As more and more empaths choose to ignore their gift,

they are becoming less connected with the universe, which has led to an increase in spiritually based hypersensitivity. Oversensitivity to people's energy and noise is a common reaction to energy acceleration, so as you ascend to greater heights in your spiritual development, you should expect to experience this. When you begin to accelerate in the spiritual realm, you may feel like a radio receiver picking up a million signals at once. When there is a shift in spiritual vibration, your sense of intuition and your empathic channels are open, causing a heightened awareness of the thoughts and feelings of those around you. Spiritual hypersensitivity can manifest physically causing third eye dizziness and hypersensitivity to energy, odors, light, and noise.

Metaphysics teaches us that the body is a vehicle for the spirit, and the body is not who we are; our person is carried in our spirit. Wayne Dyer states that we are spiritual beings living in a physical world. Everything that happens in the physical world first happens in the realm of the spirit; therefore, if there is an imbalance in your spirit, it will manifest through your physical body. Metaphysical wellness counselors always address the spiritual aspects of healing before focusing on the physical, and it is spiritual alignment that cures the physical ailments.

HOW TO COPE WITH SPIRITUAL HYPERSENSITIVITY

When the body is overwhelmed physically, emotionally, or mentally, the fight or flight syndrome is activated and breathing becomes shallow. When you begin to experience a change in your breathing pattern, you should immediately start practicing conscious breathing. This is a technique by which you focus your attention on your breath, which will slow down your nervous system and allow you to relax. Breathe slowly, deeply, and in a rhythm while focusing your mind on being able to relax in the situation you are in. Always take a temporary retreat from any stressful situation such as family or work-related conflicts. Excusing yourself to the bathroom is a good way to do this. This will allow you to get away from the negative energy, practice your breathing techniques, and renew yourself.

THERE ARE ALSO SEVERAL OTHER SPIRITUAL HEALING TOOLS THAT YOU CAN USE:

PRAYER

Depending on what you believe in, prayer can bring comfort in an overwhelming situation. One of the most talked-about and effective prayers is the Ho'oponopono prayer. Here is the story behind it:

The Hawaii State Hospital for the criminally insane was a clinic for those who had committed the most heinous of crimes. Criminals who had committed murder, kidnapping, rape, or other crimes of such magnitude were either sent there because of their mental condition or to determine whether they were sane enough to stand trial. According to one of the nurses who worked there, it was a place with no hope; the atmosphere was so congested with evil and negativity that not even paint wanted to reside in the building and would not stick to the walls. Everything was rotting, decaying, repulsive, and terrifying. Not a day would go by without someone being physically attacked.

The doctors and nurses were bound by fear; when an inmate was walking in their direction, even though they were shackled hand and foot, the medical staff would walk as close to the walls as possible to keep away from them. However, not even shackles could stop the attacks, and so the inmates were never taken outside unless it was an absolute emergency. Staff were absent the majority of the time and would often take sick leave to escape the depressing and dangerous environment they were working in.

Every few months, a new doctor was hired because the hospital was unable to handle the inmates, but one day Dr. Stanley Hew Len entered the clinic. The nurses were not at all enthusiastic because they were convinced he would be like the rest and bombard them with his supposed superior strategy that would get the place in order, and then leave within a few months when he realized the reality of the situation he had got himself into. They soon discovered that everything about this doctor was different; he wasn't doing anything significant, but his demeanor didn't fit the environment. Where everyone else was depressed and angry, he was always naturally relaxed, cheerful, and smiling. Every so often, he would ask for the files of the inmates; he rarely saw them personally, but he would sit in his office and look over their files. To the members of staff who were interested in the way he chose to operate, he would tell them about something he referred to as Ho'oponopono. As the months went by, things started to change in the hospital; the walls were painted and the paint actually remained on the walls, which gave the place some life. The gardens were pruned, the tennis courts repaired and prisoners who ordinarily were never allowed to go outside began to play tennis with the staff. They began to allow some of the prisoners to move around without their shackles and the inmates started to take less psychotropic medication.

The shift in the atmosphere was astounding; the staff stopped taking sick leave, and where there was once a shortage of applicants, there was now a high demand to work at the clinic. Slowly, they began to release the prisoners. Dr. Hew Len was employed by the clinic for almost four years, and by the time he left, only a few inmates remained. They were eventually housed in another location because the clinic had to close; the prisoners no longer required their services.

It appeared that Dr. Hew Len didn't apply any specific technique or give the prisoners any medication. All he seemed to do was look at their files, but what he did do was heal himself with a traditional Hawaiian spiritual remedy referred to as Ho'oponopono. In Dr. Len's own words, "I was healing the part of me that created them."

While he sat in his office looking at each individual patient file, he would feel pain and empathy towards them. Dr. Len would then use what he was feeling to heal himself, taking on full responsibility for what each patient appeared to be going through. The prisoners were healed because their doctor took on their pain and healed them through himself.

Ho'oponopono is based on the belief that we create our own environment; there are no external forces responsible for what is taking place within our surroundings. If your boss is evil, you are responsible. If your children are not doing well in school, you are responsible. World wars and poverty are your responsibility. The bottom line is that the world belongs to you and it is your responsibility to take care of it. Taking responsibility doesn't mean the problems are your fault, it simply means you need to heal yourself in order to heal the situation you find distressing.

Some may agree with this theology, and to others it may appear completely nonsensical, but if you really choose to analyze it, you will find that your perception of the world is your reality. If you think the world is depressive and point-less because you choose to focus on all the negativity sur-rounding you, that's how you perceive the world. You could change it if you focused on changing yourself. Two people can live in the same environment but have completely dif-ferent experiences, simply because of their perception.

So how can you heal yourself with Ho'oponopono? There are four steps to the concept:

- **Repent:** Say you are sorry for the part that you have played in the things you perceive as evil or problematic that are surrounding you. As an em-path you can say that you are sorry for the pain that the people you have met recently are experiencing.

Whatever you feel responsible for, say you are sorry for it; feel the remorse and mean it.

- **Ask for Forgiveness:** You are probably wondering, "Well, who am I asking?" We all have our different belief systems. The majority of us, and especially empaths, believe in some kind of higher power and so that is who you ask to forgive you.

- **Gratitude:** Say thank you; there is so much power in gratitude. If you take your focus off the negative, you will find that you have so many things to be thankful for. Say thank you that you woke up this morning. Say thank you that you have eyes to see, a nose to smell, legs to walk on, that your internal organs are all in working order. Find something to say thank you for and say it continuously.

- **Love:** Love is the most powerful force in the universe. Saying the words "I love you" over and over again will bring love into your life. You can say "I love you" to your cat, your house, your car, the sky, the trees! Whatever you feel love towards, say it.

WATER

Water has extraordinary balancing and healing properties, especially during times of hypersensitivity. When consumed with consciousness, it provides inner alignment. You can balance the surrounding energy by putting a drop of water on your third eye area. When you apply water that you have energized, it leads to even more powerful results. You can energize water by praying over it or putting a word on the bottle to infuse the word's frequency into the bottle. Words such as healing, calmness, and peace work well.

Taking a hot shower works well for aura cleansing and the restoration of energetic balance. Take a shower and imagine the water washing away negative feelings, impressions, and thoughts from others and envision all the negative energy being sucked down the drain.

MINDFULNESS

This technique can pull calming energy into the body. Focus on your breath while looking at something beautiful like a rose, the sun, or the sky. You can even focus on the palms of your hands as if this is the first time you have seen them. You can redirect the attention you are paying to your feelings by focusing on something visual.

ESSENTIAL OILS

Essential oils have a calming effect and can greatly improve the anxiety associated with spiritual hypersensitivity. In 2014, the American College of Healthcare Sciences conducted a study in which 58 hospice patients were given a daily hand massage for one week using a blend of essential oils. The oil blend was made up of lavender, frankincense, and bergamot. All patients reported less depression and pain as a result of the essential oil massages. The study concluded that essential oil blend aromatherapy massages were more effective for depression and pain management than massage alone.

The following are some of the best oils for treating anxiety:

LAVENDER

Lavender oil has a relaxing and calming effect; it restores the nervous system, provides inner peace, promotes better sleep, causes a reduction in restlessness, panic attacks, irritability, and general nervous tension. Several clinical studies have proven that inhaling lavender causes an immediate reduction in anxiety and stress. One study discovered that taking lavender oil capsules orally, while watching a film that caused anxiety, led to an decrease in heart rate variation in comparison to the placebo. The study concluded that lavender had an anxiolytic effect, which means that it can inhibit anxiety.

Other studies have concluded that lavender can reduce anxiety in patients having coronary artery bypass surgery and in patients who are afraid of the dentist.

ROSE

Rose alleviates depression, anxiety, grief, shock, and panic attacks. The Iranian Red Crescent Medical Journal published a study in which a group of women experiencing their first pregnancy inhaled rose oil for 10 minutes while having a footbath. A second group of women experiencing pregnancy for the first time was also given the footbath but without the rose oil inhalation. The results revealed that a footbath combined with aromatherapy caused a reduction in anxiety in nulliparous women (those who have not had any children yet) in the active phase.

VETIVER

Vetiver oil contains reassuring, grounding, and tranquil energy. It is often used for patients experiencing trauma and helps with stabilization and self-awareness. It also has a calming effect. Vetiver oil is a nervous system tonic; it reduces hypersensitivity, jitteriness, shock, and panic attacks. The Natural Product Research published a study that examined rats with anxiety disorders and found that vetiver oil caused a reduction in anxiety.

YLANG YLANG

Ylang ylang has a calming and uplifting effect; it improves depression and anxiety due to its ability to induce optimism, cheerfulness, and courage. Ylang ylang also soothes fear, nervous palpitations, and heart agitation. It is also a sedative that helps with insomnia.

A 2006 study conducted in Korea by Geochang Provincial College found that using a combination of ylang ylang, lavender, and bergamot oil for four weeks once a day caused a reduction in blood pressure, hypertension, serum cortisol levels, and psychological stress responses.

BERGAMOT

Bergamot is one of the ingredients in Earl Grey tea and has a distinctive floral aroma and taste. Bergamot oil provides a soothing energy that reduces depression and agitation, induces relaxation, and helps with insomnia. A study conducted in 2011 discovered that the application of bergamot oil reduced anxiety, depression, blood pressure, and pulse rate.

CHAMOMILE

Chamomile oil is known for its calming effect and its ability to produce inner peace, reduce worry, anxiety, over-thinking, and irritability. The University of Pennsylvania School of Medicine conducted an explorative study and found that chamomile oil contains medicinal anti-depressant properties. The National Center for Complementary and Integrative Health also found that chamomile capsules can reduce anxiety-related symptoms.

FRANKINCENSE

Frankincense oil is great for treating anxiety and depression due to its tranquil energy and calming effects. It also helps you focus, quiet the mind, and deepen meditation. A Keimyung University study in Korea found that a combination of lavender, frankincense, and bergamot reduced pain and depression in hospice patients suffering from terminal cancer.

HOW TO USE ESSENTIAL OILS FOR HYPERSENSITIVITY

Essential oils are either ingested, applied topically, or used in aromatherapy. Here are some suggestions for their usage:

AROMATHERAPY

Aromatherapy is a very popular remedy for anxiety because of the human ability to process information through smell; it can trigger a very powerful emotional response. There is a region in the brain called the limbic system that controls memory recall and emotional processing. Inhaling the scent of essential oils stimulates a mental response in the brain's limbic system, which regulates stress and promotes calming responses such as the production of relaxation hormones, decreased blood pressure, and regular breathing patterns. You can use the oils in the bath, a hot water vapor, a humidifier or vaporizer, cologne, perfume, a vent, aromatherapy diffusers, or through direct inhalation.

ORAL APPLICATION

You can consume the majority of essential oils orally. However, the oils you use must be safe and pure. The majority of commercialized oils have been blended with synthetics or diluted with other substances, making them unsafe for ingesting. The most effective method for consuming essential oils is to combine a drop of oil with a teaspoon of honey or drop the oil into a glass of water. You can also add a couple of drops to the food you are cooking. You can place a couple of drops under your tongue. This is particularly beneficial because the blood capillaries are located under the tongue near the surface of the tissue, which allows the oil to quickly be absorbed into the bloodstream and travel to the area of the body where it is required. You can also take essential oils in capsule form.

TOPICAL APPLICATION

Topical application is the process of placing essential oils on the skin, nails, teeth, hair, or mucous membranes of the body. The oils are quickly absorbed by the skin. Due to the strength of the oils, you must dilute or blend them with a carrier oil such as coconut, avocado, jojoba, or sweet almond oil. You can apply the blended mixture directly to the affected area, around the rims of the ears, the soles of the feet, in the bath, through a warm compress, or through a massage.

To learn more about how to optimize essential oils in your life, refer to the end of the book where I've included four high-quality essential oil recipes to relieve anxiety.

CHAPTER 5:

EMPATHS, INSOMNIA, EXHAUSTION, AND ADRENAL FATIGUE

D ue to the emotional responsibilities that empaths carry, they often experience a sudden drop in energy, which leads to chronic fatigue. When an empath does not remain grounded, balanced, and consciously aware, they can unconsciously give their energy to others. When an empath spends too much time in the company

of negative or depressed people, they take on their energy, and this can lead to emotional exhaustion. This is one of the main reasons they must spend time alone as a way of recharging their internal batteries.

The mind, soul, and body are connected, so whatever we think and feel affects our physical body. An empath must have regular periods of isolation throughout the day in order to process feelings and emotions. This prevents emotional exhaustion, which then enables them to constantly let go of crushing negative energy. If an empath does not do this, they find it difficult to sleep at night because their minds are unable to process and make sense of the information they absorbed during the day. This hyperactive mindset causes empaths to become extremely tired. If the empath can't find solitude during the day, they must meditate before they go to bed so they can release any extreme emotions they have come into contact with throughout the day.

EFFECTS OF THE ADRENAL GLANDS

Negative feelings can lead to the empath experiencing fear, resentment, anxiety, paranoia, and panic, and becoming genuinely convinced that something bad is going to happen to them. These thoughts send signals to the adrenal glands, which produce hormones that release excess amounts of energy. Not enough sleep, too much work, bad diet, bad relationships, and family problems all have a negative effect on the adrenal glands. The adrenal glands are shaped like the kidneys but are approximately the size of a walnut. They are located just above the kidneys in the lower back area. The adrenal glands are of great benefit when we are under stress because they assist in keeping us focused and alert and they increase our levels of stamina, which enables us to better handle pressure.

However, when the adrenal glands are overstimulated, they continue to produce energy, which is what prevents us from being able to sleep. The mind and body stay on high alert, which causes excess stress on the adrenal glands and will eventually cause them to malfunction. A lack of energy leads to a craving for foods that are high in sugar and refined salt, which quickly turn into energy, giving the body an instant but short-lived energy boost.

The body naturally craves sugar and salt. However, we tend to feed it with refined sugar and salt, which is found in the majority of junk and processed foods. In excess amounts, these foods can cause a range of different health problems. Unrefined sugar and salt are nutritious in healthy doses and can replenish and nourish the adrenal glands.

When the adrenal glands are not functioning properly, you will feel tired, groggy, anxious, irritable, overwhelmed, and dizzy. You may also experience heart palpitations, high or low blood pressure, salt and sugar cravings as well as find it difficult to handle stress. If our bodies are in harmony, we are eating a good diet, sleeping well and having positive thoughts, the adrenal glands are not so easily overwhelmed. Cortisol is a hormone produced by the adrenal glands; during sleep our cortisol levels rise and peak a few hours before daybreak. This is how the body naturally prepares itself for the day and it is referred to as the circadian rhythm. It increases our energy levels, so we are capable of functioning throughout the day. When the adrenal glands are overworked, we wake up feeling exhausted even if we have had the normal eight hours of sleep. We feel tired throughout the day, which then causes our cortisol levels to peak in the evening, making it hard for us to sleep properly.

KEEPING THE ADRENAL GLANDS HEALTHY

It takes a long time to destroy the adrenal glands, and it will take the same amount of time to repair them. However, there are some changes that we can make in our lives that will help immediately. We must spend time listening to our body so we are aware of how it feels at any given moment. This allows us to keep track of our energy levels throughout the day. You may find that your energy levels fluctuate throughout the day and that there are certain times when your energy levels drop the most. You must understand what is causing so much stress to the adrenal glands. When the root cause of the problem is identified, we can ensure that we don't remain in that heightened state and put further strain on the adrenal glands.

Meditation is a powerful tool for emptying the mind and spirit of negative emotions. It also helps us focus on the body so that we are aware of any physical sensations taking place. When we feel isolated, lonely, and separated, cortisol levels can increase; you can combat this situation by spending time with friends and family. However, if you are the type of person who likes spending time alone and you enjoy your own company, periods of isolation should not be a problem.

Let's move on to explore some key physical factors and fixes related to empaths, fatigue and quality of sleep. First of all, diet and exercise can have a negative effect on the adrenal gland. It is not a good idea to push too hard during a workout; your body will tell you when it has had enough, and it is essential that you stop at this point or you will cause the adrenal glands to produce excess stress-related hormones.

Eating junk food, skipping meals and doing hardcore workouts all cause the adrenal glands to overwork. To keep the adrenal glands in a healthy state, we should eat an or-ganic, nutritional, and well-balanced diet with the daily protein requirements, and vitamins A, B, and C. Refrain from excess alcohol and preferably eliminate refined salt, sugar, and caffeine. A healthy state of mind where you feel peaceful and content with life, and are getting enough sleep at night all contribute to healthy adrenal glands.

WHY CUT OUT REFINED SALT?

Research conducted by the director of the University of Washington in Seattle found that low sodium levels cause a reduction in blood volume. The body compensates by activating the sympathetic nervous system, which releases adrenaline, triggering the fight or flight response, which makes sleep difficult.

WHY CUT OUT REFINED SUGAR?

When the adrenals are overworked, it can cause interrupted sleep patterns, often from vivid dreams, all of which can cause heightened anxiety. Stress and anxiety contribute to sleepless nights due to excess adrenaline; this typically takes place between 2:00 and 4:00 a.m. The surge of hormones makes it difficult for us to remain calm and wakes the body up in an agitated state.

Here is a natural remedy that will assist in eliminating this problem:

HONEY AND SALT

Combine five teaspoons of raw organic honey with 1 teaspoon of Himalayan rock salt. Twenty minutes before going to bed, place a small amount under the tongue and let it dissolve. The combination of salt and honey naturally de-stresses the body through hormone regulation. This results in a harmonious, peaceful, and restful state, which prepares the body for deep sleep. Honey and salt also sustain the body, preventing you from waking up feeling hungry during the night.

Those who consume honey and salt before going to bed have reported that they no longer experience sleep deprivation; they sleep throughout the night and wake up energized and refreshed and no longer experience dips in energy throughout the day. Bedtime anxiety is replaced with the peace and tranquility that comes with knowing they will be asleep within minutes and remain in a sound, smooth sleep until morning.

THE BENEFITS OF RAW ORGANIC HONEY

Honey aids in releasing liver glycogen in the brain. A lack of liver glycogen causes the adrenal glands to produce the stress hormones cortisol and adrenaline. One of the ingredients in honey is tryptophan, which is responsible for producing serotonin, a hormone that induces relaxation. When there is no light, serotonin is converted to melatonin, which causes restorative sleep.

Melatonin regulates the sleep-wake cycle as it works in harmony with the morning and night. When our melatonin levels are stable, we fall asleep easily and naturally when it gets dark, and when light starts to enter the room, our body automatically wakes up.

We have been taught to believe that salt is bad for our health, but this statement is not entirely true. A healthy balance of the right salt stabilizes the metabolism. We must have a healthy metabolism, as it ensures the food we eat is absorbed and turned into energy. Salt contains anti-excitatory and anti-stress properties, which reduces our stress levels and helps us remain calm.

We often have a craving for salt, not realizing that it eliminates anxiety and creates an overall sense of well-being. Unfortunately, when this need arises, the majority of us consume processed foods containing refined table salts, which have no health benefits. When we start consuming unrefined salts such as Celtic, Himalayan, or Real salt, we immediately notice that our stress levels go down, our energy levels are increased, and we have a clear mental and emotional state.

Another myth is that eating after 7 p.m. causes weight gain; there is no scientific evidence to support this. However, there is evidence to suggest that an evening snack helps us stay asleep because when we get hungry, the adrenal stress hormone is activated by the brain, which then puts us on the fight or flight alert.

BENEFITS OF A HIMALAYAN SALT LAMP

A Himalayan salt lamp is a huge piece of pure Himalayan salt with a small bulb on the inside. It provides a subtle warm glow that improves the quality of the air. Mobile phones and laptops release an overload of positive ions into the air. An ion is a molecule or atom in which the sum of the electrons is not equal to the sum of the protons; this gives the atom a net negative or positive electrical charge. A Himalayan salt lamp will balance out the ions, making you feel happier and creating a sense of calmness and freshness in the air.

Positive charged ions are also referred to as cations, and negative charged ions are also referred to as anions. The combination of negative and positive charged ions enables them to bond and move around in the atmosphere. Positive ions are generated by electronic devices such as microwaves, TVs, computers, and vacuum cleaners. They can cause and intensify health problems such as sleep deprivation, allergies, and stress. Negative ions are typically created by sunlight, lightning storms, ocean waves, and waterfalls. According to Pierce J. Howard, the author of *The Owner's Manual for the Brain*, there are several benefits associated with negative ions. They cause more oxygen to flow to the brain, which results in less drowsiness, more mental energy, and alertness. They protect against germs in the atmosphere that can cause sneezing, throat irritation, and coughing. One in three people is sensitive to the effects of negative ions and they can make people feel refreshed instantly.

The best way to get negative ion exposure is to spend time outdoors, especially around water. Himalayan salt lamps produce small amounts of negative ions. Negative and positive ions bond together, which causes the negative ions to neutralize the positive ions. This process helps to cleanse the air. Salt lamps also provide a soft glow, which many people find relaxing.

Salt is hygroscopic, which means that it pulls water to the surface so that it quickly evaporates due to the heat emitted from the light bulb. This is one of the reasons salt lamps leak water in humid climates. When there is water vapor in the air, it carries bacteria, mold, and allergens. Salt lamps draw the water vapor, as well as the elements it is carrying, to the surface of the lamp, thereby removing it from the air. This is one of the most beneficial functions of a salt lamp.

A LOW-LAMP LIGHT MAKES A GREAT NIGHT LIGHT

According to research, the body is affected by different colors of light. It is recommended that blue light be avoided after the sun goes down because it can have a negative effect on the circadian rhythm, which disrupts sleep hormones.

The majority of light sources such as tablets, laptops, computers, TVs, and cell phones emit blue light and most of us spend hours on end staring at these screens, especially during the evening.

Salt lamps provide a warm orange light similar to the light that radiates from candlelight or a campfire. This is why they are a beneficial light source and can stay on throughout the night without interrupting sleep.

For those who suffer from seasonal affective disorder (SAD), soft orange hues increase focus, boost energy levels, and calm moods. The negative ions also contain mood-enhancing elements.

CHAPTER 6:

HOW TO PROTECT YOURSELF FROM ENERGY VAMPIRES

An energy vampire is a person who drains your energy; they are also referred to as energy suckers and psychic vampires. Some energy vampires are conscious of what they are doing while others are not. The unconscious ones are typically mentally ill or emotionally unstable; they have a desperate need to draw life from those

who have healthy and strong energy. Empaths will usually feel dizzy or drained when energy is being drawn from them by a vampire.

There are also conscious energy vampires who have been trained by negative and dark forces to collect positive energy. They do this for several reasons: to gain recognition and power, boost their self-esteem, boost their ego, or for youth-seeking or health reasons.

You must protect yourself from energy drainers. Here are some strategies to help you:

DON'T GIVE TOO MUCH

It is good to give, as it enhances your psychic awareness, spiritual growth, and your personal evolution. However, you must replenish yourself every time you give; you need to master the balance of giving and receiving. When someone gives you something small, like paying you a compliment, receive it with an open heart and say thank you; there is no need to give back to them and respond with another compliment.

REFRAIN FROM PEOPLE PLEASING

Some people will attempt to please everyone. This is simply not possible; we all have different frequency vibrations. You will attract those with whom you are on a similar vibration and the others you will deflect. You can be your own energy vampire when you attempt to please everyone.

Be Cautious of Egotistical People

People who are only focused on themselves will drain you. When you have a conversation with them, all they can talk about is what they are doing and will ask how you are just as you are about to part ways. You will feel drained at the end of a conversation with them; limit your contact with or completely remove such people from your life.

Be Cautious of Needy People

Needy people do anything and everything to get your attention. They are constantly asking for your help and advice but never apply it. These people will waste your time and drain your energy. Train yourself to recognize when you are dealing with such people and reduce the amount of contact that you have with them.

Be Careful of Drama Queens

These people are not difficult to detect because they are always involved in some type of problem. Everything that could go wrong does, and they are constantly bombarding you with emails, phone calls, and text messages about the latest catastrophe in their life. Before you realize it, you will have no energy left. You mustn't waste your time engaging with such people because they will destroy your field of energy.

Clarity

Don't waste time beating around the bush with people, get straight to the point. When a person is being too negative, shut them down; when a person keeps operating in the same behaviors and then asking for your advice, shut them down. If someone asks you to do something for them and you can't do it, just say so. You don't need to be rude, just be firm and let people know what your boundaries are so that they don't cross them.

HERB SMUDGING

Smudging involves the process of burning herbs to create a bath of cleansing smoke for the purpose of protection, purification, and healing. Palo Santo Wood, also referred to as Holy Wood, is a type of sacred wood used by the indigenous people of the Andes and the shamans in Peru for purifying, medicinal purposes, and to remove evil spirits. You can use cedar, sage, and pine for smudging.

GEMSTONES AND CRYSTALS OR GEM ELIXIRS

Quartz crystals, tiger eye, amethyst, tourmaline, obsidian, and onyx are all used to protect against emotional distress, danger, psychic attack, empathy, and oversensitivity.

ORGONE

Orgone has several functions, including creating a protective energy field that surrounds your environment and your aura, and deflecting negative energy. It is also used as a shield to deflect harmful pollutants and electromagnetic frequencies.

Place four orgone protectors in the four corners of your home to protect against harmful energy and ground spiritual energies. The Orgone Amulet of Protection protects against psychic attacks, bad vibes, emotional pollution, and evil eye.

CANDLES

Candles remove negative energy from your home. They are also excellent for manifesting purposes. Dark blue, red, and white candles are good colors to use for self-protection.

RESINS AND INCENSE

Incense made from natural substances such as frankincense, myrrh, sage, sandalwood, and musk can be used to cleanse the atmosphere of homes and environments.

BATHS

Add ½ cup of sea salt to your bath; this will cleanse any negative energy that has attached itself to you. Steep a teaspoon of clove or basil into a cup of boiling water, strain the herbs, and add it to your bath; these herbs are known for their cleansing and protecting properties.

PROTECTION PRAYERS AND CHANTS

Any chants or prayers will work, as long as they come from the heart with intensity, passion, and determination.

CHAPTER 7:

EMPATHS AND WORK

As an empath, you will face particular challenges in the workplace. Everyone deserves a job that fits their abilities and personality, but you need to take extra care before accepting a position because a toxic work environment can make you emotionally, spiritually, and physically sick — fast. So, as an empath, how can you pick the right kind of job and thrive at work?

ALWAYS ASK FOR A WORKPLACE TOUR BEFORE ACCEPTING A ROLE

When you go for an interview, ask whether you can take a tour if someone hasn't already offered to show you around. Pay attention to the employees' facial expressions, their body language, and the way they talk to one another. You'll quickly surmise whether the organization is toxic. Unless you are in desperate need of money, follow your gut instinct and avoid workplaces that contain a significant amount of negative energy.

Pay close attention to the lighting, the noise levels, the amount of clutter, and the layout of the desks. Ask yourself whether you would be comfortable working in such an environment, from both a physical and emotional perspective. A high salary might be enticing, but your health and sanity must come first. Even if other people tell you that a job is too good an opportunity to pass up, trust your intuition.

You have the power to make a positive difference in the workplace, but you are under no obligation to sacrifice your mental and physical health if doing so is beyond your comfort zone. Never feel bad about choosing the right job for you.

USE YOUR GIFT AS A SELLING POINT

Empaths are not show-offs by nature, and the prospect of selling yourself in a job interview might be enough to make you feel queasy. But think of it this way – your empathic qualities are actually an increasingly valuable commodity in the workplace. We tend to associate the business world, and even the public sector, with a kind of cut-throat mentality where everyone is trying to outdo one another and compete for the best positions and the most money.

However, our society is increasingly aware that taking care of one another and our planet is the only way forward. We still have a long way to go in terms of creating a more caring world, but in general, we are starting to understand the benefit of a healthy work-life balance and the merits of cooperative working practices rather than a dog-eat-dog mentality. If you feel up to the challenge, you can use your gift to help drive this change!

You know that there is far more to life – and work – than status or salary. Your gift makes you perfectly suited to roles that require listening, conflict resolution, and mentoring skills. Psychiatrist, author, and empath Dr. Judith Orloff maintains that empaths bring passion, excellent communication skills, and leadership ability to their professional roles. When an interviewer asks what you can bring to a job, don't hesitate to give examples of times you have demonstrated these gifts.

WORKING ALONE VERSUS WORKING WITH OTHERS

Although you have strong leadership potential, a role involving extensive contact with colleagues and customers on a day-to-day basis may prove too draining, especially if you are not yet confident in your ability to handle negative energy and toxic individuals. Be honest with yourself when applying for a position. If it entails working as part of a busy team with few opportunities to recharge during the day, think carefully before making an application.

Most empaths are well suited to working for themselves or taking on jobs within small organizations. Working in a large office or noisy environment may be too stimulating – and that's fine! We all have different needs and talents, so do not allow anyone to make you feel inferior for not being able to handle a "normal" workplace. As an empath, you may quickly become overwhelmed by the prospect of having to interact constantly with coworkers, members of the management team, and customers.

On the other hand, working alone can result in social isolation if you take it to extremes. If you decide to run a small business from home, for example, be sure to schedule some time with family and friends at least a couple of times each week.

Not only do you need to nurture your relationships, but it is also helpful to gain an outsider's perspective on your work from time to time. Sometimes you may get so caught up in a project that relatively minor problems seem to take on a life of their own. Talking to other people allows you to take a more realistic view and helps you come up with new solutions.

IF YOUR ENVIRONMENT DRAINS YOUR ENERGY, ASK FOR REASONABLE ADJUSTMENTS

You can't expect your boss to redecorate the office just to suit your preferences or to fire an energy vampire, but you can ask them politely whether they would mind making a few small adjustments. For example, if there is a harsh strip light directly over your desk, you could ask whether it would be possible to turn off the light and use softer, gentler lamps instead.

If you work in an environment in which people talk loudly, experiment with white noise or other sound recordings designed to trigger feelings of calm and emotional stability. Try sounds recorded in nature, as these are often soothing for empaths. You can find lots of free resources on YouTube or specialized noise-generating sites such as mynoise.net. If possible, listen to natural or white noise via noise-cancellation headphones for at least a portion of your workday.

There are also additions and adjustments you can make that do not require permission from your boss. For instance, you can place crystals on your desk as a means of countering negative energy and set aside a few minutes each day – even if you are incredibly busy – to ensure your desk is clear of unnecessary clutter. If you work with a computer, pick a calming scene or color as your desktop screensaver. Frame a photo or uplifting picture and keep it on your desk. Look at it for a few seconds when you need a dose of positive energy.

If you enjoy your job but would prefer to spend less time around other people, consider asking your manager whether you can work from home a couple of days each week. This can give you some respite from other peoples' energy and enables you to take a break at any time. Working from home comes with the privilege of setting up an environment that suits you perfectly. For example, you could install a water feature on your desk or play natural background noise throughout the day without fear of eliciting annoying questions from your coworkers.

WATCH OUT FOR ENERGY VAMPIRES

If you come across an energy vampire in your personal life, you usually have the option of cutting contact with them, or at least limiting how much time the two of you spend hanging out. Unfortunately, this isn't the case when you are forced to work alongside them.

This is where boundaries come into play. You need to politely but firmly assert yourself from the outset. Don't be drawn into petty workplace gossip, and don't accept any invitations from toxic people to socialize outside of work. Draw on your best energy self-defense skills, and always put your well-being before professional obligations.

Empaths who choose to work in the helping professions, whether with other people or animals, need to remain aware of the effect of their work on their energy levels. For example, if you work as a psychologist or therapist, speaking to a client who is going through an especially sad or difficult time in their life can leave you exhausted, depleted, and even depressed. Be sure to allow a few minutes between clients or appointments in which to ground yourself, and schedule plenty of time to relax and nurture yourself outside of work.

DRAW A LINE BETWEEN YOUR WORKPLACE AND HOME

If you work outside the home, it's a good idea to devise a routine that creates a clear dividing line between your professional and personal life. As an empath, you are susceptible to carrying the negative energy of others with you. You may catch yourself worrying not only about the problems you are facing at work, but also those of your colleagues, bosses, and customers. Unless you learn how to "switch off," you will soon become overwhelmed, anxious, and depressed.

When it's time to wrap up your work for the day, stay mindful of the transition between work and home. Create a ritual that automatically encourages you to switch your focus to personal interests and feelings rather than those of colleagues and clients. For example, you may wish to spend the final five minutes of your workday in meditation or tidying your desk while listening to a particular soundtrack or piece of music. If you have a friend or relative who always raises your energy levels, you could get into the habit of texting them just before leaving work or on the way home.

Focus On How Your Work Helps Others

It isn't always possible to change your job or work in the field of your choosing. If you are stuck in a job that isn't right for you and are in no position to make a change any time soon, try approaching your work with a new mindset.

As an empath, you have a talent for helping others. Not only do they benefit from your support, but you also get to soak up their positive energy too. It's truly a win-win situation! Try to find opportunities to lend a hand to someone else and offer emotional support, as long as it doesn't leave you feeling too drained.

For example, if one of your colleagues seems especially stressed, take the initiative and ask them if they'd like to talk to you for five minutes about anything that's bothering them. Sometimes, just offering a listening ear can turn someone's day around! Or perhaps you could offer a more practical form of help. For instance, you could offer to take everyone's mail to the mailroom on your coffee break. Acts of service and kindness allow you to find a sense of meaning in your work, even if you are hoping to change careers in the near future.

CHAPTER 8:

NORMALIZING AND MAINTAINING YOUR GIFT

Now you have learned how to embrace and leverage your gift, the next step is to normalize it. This involves learning how to make the gift a normal part of everyday life. At this stage, you will no longer need to think about how you plan on responding, or how you intend to use your gift, you will just be able to use it and reap the benefits. There will be no need to put any effort into thinking about tapping into your gift; it will become like the air that you breathe.

The normalizing process is a crucial part of fully stepping into your gift as an empath. It will free you from worrying about the fact that you are an empath because now you are capable of managing it consistently. Never again will you have to worry that your gift has some type of hold over you because you now know what you need to do when things get out of control. You will be able to tune in and out of energy when you want to.

You will never become void of all the emotions that you used to feel; when you are normalized, you will only feel the emotions and energy that you want to feel. You will no longer automatically pick up energy from other people or feel an immediate negative reaction to the energies you are exposed to. Once upon a time, you might have lost your temper or become exhausted and drained because of negative energy. You may have avoided crowds, public places, certain people, dinner parties, family gatherings, and housewarming parties because you knew that you would leave feeling drained, overwhelmed, and exhausted, which could last for several days. During that time, you were perplexed as to where these feelings were coming from, leading you to feel frustrated and irritated.

Now you have become accustomed to life as an empath, you no longer experience these negative feelings. You can walk into a room full of unfamiliar or familiar people and feel energized and empowered. You no longer absorb the emotions and energies of other people; you are still capable of reading their emotions, but they no longer have the power to hold you hostage. You know how to ground yourself and deflect the feelings, energy, and emotions that are not beneficial to you.

MAINTAIN YOUR GIFT

Maintaining and mastering your gift are two completely different processes. When you have mastered your gift, you find it easy to live in harmony with it, and as discussed above, you have normalized it. However, don't get comfortable once you have reached the normalization stage because now you need to maintain your gift to ensure you don't regress. There are several things you will need to do to maintain your gift. This process will enable you to live in perfect harmony with your gift.

REGULAR CHECK-INS

To maintain your gift, you must check in regularly. You should do this a minimum of once a day, but you should really aim for twice a day. The best times to do so are first thing in the morning and before you go to bed. This will enable you to reflect on the things that have had the most effect on you throughout the day. In the morning, you are capable of recognizing residual experiences that you have been unconsciously holding onto. Much of what attaches itself to our minds often comes to life in our dreams; you can then let these feelings go and get on with your day in peace and harmony.

It is a good idea to check in before going to bed because the experiences you have had throughout the day will be fresh in your mind. You will be able to detect how these experiences have affected you and release them so you can have a peaceful and restful sleep.

Daily Meditation

The best time to meditate is as soon as you wake up in the morning and just before you are going to bed at night. However, make sure that you don't make a habit of meditating until you fall asleep because this can have a negative effect on your meditation practices. It can leave an imprint on your unconscious mind causing you to associate meditation with sleeping, which will lead you to fall asleep during your meditation times in the morning and throughout the day. Meditating gives you the opportunity to rest with your energy. You don't have to feel as if you are in control; there is no stress, and you can enjoy your energy at that moment.

Deep Breathing

It is important that you relax often, but at the same time, you should make sure that your breathing follows a certain pattern. Deep breathing allows you to relax completely by achieving a state of rest within your body. A good breathing exercise is to breathe in for 4 seconds, hold your breath for 6 seconds, and then breathe out for 8 seconds. This will help eliminate any excess air from your body. Imagine any negative energy or stress leaving your body with the air.

Deep breathing is an excellent way of centering yourself and quickly gaining harmony within. If you ever find yourself struggling with your grounding exercise, begin to intentionally center your breathing. This will help you gain complete control over your emotions and come back to your power center. It is advised that you practice breathing deeply daily and anytime you find yourself in a distressing situation.

INTENTIONAL GROUNDING

An important part of normalizing your abilities as an empath is that you ground and shield yourself on a regular basis. The process of grounding allows you to regularly eliminate unwanted energy and intentionally come back to your center.

You should never leave maintaining your energy on autopilot because you will fall out of alignment very quickly and become unbalanced. Even when you have managed to master your abilities as an empath, you will still find that you get into situations where you are absorbing energy from other people.

CHAPTER 9:

HOW TO SUPPORT A YOUNG EMPATH

You now know how to take care of yourself as an empath, and how to best use your gift. However, if you have a young empath in your life, it's important that you also understand how to support them. Children with this ability often face significant challenges, but your support can make all the difference as they come to terms with the fact that they are a bit different from their peers.

Being an empathic child is tough, but young empaths have so much to offer our world, and they should be appreciated! Psychologist and empathy expert Dr. Michele Borba believes teenagers today are running low on empathy. In fact, they are only half as empathic as those of previous generations. It's clear that young empaths have a lot to teach their peers.

How To Spot a Young Empath

Empathic gifts are present from birth, and young empaths have the same abilities and needs as empathic adults. However, because children have less experience with understanding and expressing their emotions, their empathic nature may manifest in a different way.

Empathic children usually prefer to play alone or in the company of just one or two good friends. In general, they gain more enjoyment from talking and playing with older children and adults than those their own age. It isn't that they believe themselves to be superior to their classmates. Rather, a young empath's unusual maturity means that they are on the same wavelength as those older than themselves. They may report feeling distant or alienated from people their own age.

An empathic child may surprise you with their uncanny ability to home in on what others are thinking and feeling. For example, you may be feeling stressed about an incident at work while cooking dinner for the family one evening. Your empath child might walk past the kitchen door and immediately discern that you are upset about something that has happened during the day. They may well give you a hug and ask you to tell them exactly what or who has made you sad.

You must strike a balance between honoring their gift and overloading them with inappropriate information. If you are upset or angry, denying it will teach your child that their intuition cannot be trusted, which will instill self-doubt and confusion.

On the other hand, there is no need to share too many details, as this could cause a child unnecessary distress. For example, a young child does not need to know absolutely everything about a serious illness or assault. A simple acknowledgment of the situation and the feelings that go with it will be sufficient in most cases. Do not lie to your child and keep discussions age appropriate.

UNCOVER THE REAL REASONS BEHIND TEMPER TANTRUMS

Think carefully before chastising a young empath for bad behavior. Yes, they might be disobeying you simply because they are a naughty child, but they could also be acting out in response to overwhelming stimuli in their environment.

Consider the situation from a toddler's perspective. As an empathic adult, you can usually make your excuses and leave if you find yourself bombarded by too much noise or light. Unfortunately, a young child has less autonomy and often has no choice but to endure it. In a bid to protect themselves, they may either freeze up – which is why empathic children are often labeled "shy"– or they can attempt to regain control over the situation by causing their own noise and disturbance!

If you suspect that your child is an empath, do not be surprised if they suddenly act out from time to time. If they are having meltdowns or tantrums on a regular basis, it's time to dig a little deeper. Think like a detective. Are there any triggers that reliably predict "bad" behavior? Take your child's complaints seriously – if they tell you that they don't like strong light or smells, believe them!

Let anyone else who cares for your child know that they are an empath or, if this concept is alien to the person in question, that your child is unusually sensitive and re-quires a few minor adjustments. For example, if they attend a daycare center, you should let the staff know that they are liable to become overwhelmed during high-energy games and might require some time out to calm themselves down.

Under no circumstances should you shout at a young empath, use harsh punishments, or resort to abusive tac-tics such as name-calling. These approaches are destructive anyway, but when the child in question is an empath, they are likely to cause long-lasting damage. If you lose your temper, apologize immediately. Take full responsibility for your conduct.

CREATE SOOTHING ENVIRONMENTS

Make sure that an empathic child has a safe space they can call their own, and allow them to retreat when they need some alone time in which to relax and recharge their batteries. If they need to spend ten or twenty minutes in their room then let them, even if you have family or friends over.

Empathic children may require more time to wind down and get ready for sleep at the end of a busy day. Their nervous systems are more easily stimulated than those of typical children, and just telling them to get into bed and close their eyes is unlikely to result in a good night's rest!

It's a good idea to schedule a bedtime routine to help them relax. For example, you could prepare them a bath with calming essential oils, tell them a familiar bedtime story, and encourage them to reflect on the best things that happened that day.

HELP THEM PREPARE FOR THE HARSHER REALITIES OF LIFE

Caring for an empathic child can be heartbreaking at times because their gentle, kind hearts are easily bruised when they realize how much suffering exists in the world. They are also more susceptible to hurt feelings if and when an argument breaks out in their social circle. An empathic child might struggle to understand why other children seem to hurt one another because they themselves could never behave in such a cruel manner.

It's natural and normal, as a parent or caregiver, to try to shield a child from pain. Unfortunately, although it may work in the short term, you will be doing them a disservice in the long run. An empath who is not taught how to work with their gift and handle their emotions early in life is at risk of depression, anxiety, and confusion later on when they come up against the harsh realities of the world.

You cannot solve the world's problems, but you can keep the lines of communication open with your child. When they pick up on signs of tension and emotional turmoil, whether it's at home or school, give them the chance to talk about it. Encourage them to express themselves fully – feelings are there to be felt, after all. It's far healthier to teach them coping strategies early on. This empowers them because they know they can handle almost anything life throws their way.

GIVE THEM PRACTICAL TECHNIQUES THEY CAN USE

So how can you equip a young empath with the tools they need to thrive in a harsh world?

First, teach them how to meditate, and the importance of taking at least a few minutes each day to ground themselves. Children are more receptive to new ideas than adults, and you probably won't have to spend much time and energy persuading them to try it out. Why not schedule joint meditation time each day? This will not only help them develop a positive habit that will last a lifetime, but it will also deepen your bond.

Second, help them learn to verbalize their emotions, to give them a name, and understand how others' feelings exert a direct effect on their moods. Emphasize that it's important to choose healthy friends who are usually happy, and to spend time with people who leave them feeling energized instead of down.

Unfortunately, empaths of all ages are favorite targets for energy vampires and abusers of all kinds. Teach your young empath how to build boundaries, to set their own standards for relationships, and to walk away from people who wish them harm. Make a point of telling them that they can always come to you if they want or need advice on how to handle a toxic friend or bully. Practice saying "No," and use role-playing to rehearse how your child can extricate themselves from difficult situations.

Model the kind of behavior you want to see in your child. Do not deny your own feelings, make time for yourself when you get overwhelmed, and draw firm boundaries when others try to take advantage of you. Children are keen observers, and they look to their parents and caregivers for guidance.

If you are living in a home where two or more people frequently get into fights, take steps to address the problem. Young empaths pick up on tension in their living environment, and this can result in serious psychological and physical illness. Family counseling may be necessary in some situations.

TEENAGE EMPATHS

The teen years are challenging for almost everyone, and they pose special challenges for empaths. It is natural and normal for teens to seek acceptance from their peers, to break away from their families, and create their own identities. It is normal to experience heightened, turbulent emotions during this period. However, normal teenage problems can spiral into long-lasting psychological turmoil for an unsupported young empath.

Peer pressure is a real problem for teenagers. In their desire to gain their peers' approval, they may agree to take part in risky activities such as drinking, smoking, underage sex, and reckless driving. Fear of peer rejection can drive even mature empaths to put themselves in danger. For their protection, they must understand the importance of strong boundaries and saying "No." If they haven't developed this ability by the time they enter adolescence, don't worry. It's never too late to learn.

Depression, anxiety, and other mental health problems often surface for the first time in adolescence. This means that young empaths may have to deal not only with their own mental health problems but also those of their friends. As naturally caring individuals, they will feel inclined to offer a listening ear or shoulder to cry on. This is an admirable response, but the young empath can soon feel overwhelmed by the sheer strength of a friend's emotions.

A transparent, nonjudgmental approach is best. Educate your teen about the difference between normal teenage emotions and adolescent mental health problems. Teach them how to spot signs of mental illness in themselves and others and tell them where and how to get help. Bear in mind that they might not feel comfortable talking to you, so tell them that you will not be offended if they choose to seek guidance elsewhere.

If they are supporting a friend, praise their kindness but, at the same time, emphasize the importance of setting personal boundaries. If their friend is draining their emotional reservoirs, it's time to point them in the direction of professional help. Reassure your teen that they cannot be expected to "save" their friend and, sometimes, calling on the services of a qualified adult is the best step to take.

In summary, the early years of an empath's life are key to their well-being as adults. Young empaths quickly realize that they hold special abilities. If they are not supported by the adults around them, an empath can feel lonely or even alienated from others. Fortunately, with gentle guidance and nurturing, they will come to appreciate and enjoy their amazing gift.

CONCLUSION

There is much more to being an empath than what you have read in this part of the book. This is only the tip of the iceberg. Your journey has just begun, and you will continue to grow in your gift, meet others, and read more to enhance your knowledge. When you are unable to control your gift, it can often feel like a curse; after all, who wants to feel continuously drained, unwell, and exhausted? It can be difficult for you to manage at first, but as you learn to embrace and have power over your gift, you will eventually learn how to use it to leverage and enhance your life. You may even decide to use your gift to better the lives of others. Many empaths use their gifts directly in a career and others prefer to be more secretive or subtle about it. Whatever you choose to do is up to you, and there is no right or wrong way to use your gift. The most important thing is that you understand that you are not crazy, there is nothing wrong with you, and that you can live a happy and healthy life.

It is important not to get offended by people who don't understand your gift because it really isn't their fault. Unless the person is an empath, they will find it difficult to comprehend. People will judge you and accuse you of being overly emotional and sensitive, which isn't wrong, but when it is said in a demeaning way, it can be hurtful. You must learn to protect yourself against the unwanted energy from these comments.

I hope that you now have a better understanding of your gift and that you embrace every part of it so your life is enriched day by day.

I wish you all the best on your journey!

PART 2

INTRODUCTION

et's call Part 1 the warm-up; a bit like how you perform stretching exercises before starting the real workout. In it, I touched on subjects like anxiety, maintaining your gift, your work environment, and protection prayers. Part 2 goes into a bit more detail and provides loads of helpful tips and strategies for unblocking chakras, dealing with anxiety, protecting your energy, managing negative emotions, and much more.

Before you get into this, just a quick word of advice… as with all things in life, you get out of it what you put in. The road called "easy" doesn't exist; it's a figment of your imagination. If it did exist, we would probably have world peace right now because all empaths would be operating from their highest selves. If you want to sharpen your empath gift, you've got to put the work in. In chapter 6, I talk about superheroes and their superpower: every superhero has to practice their gift before it becomes a superpower and they can start using it effectively. Your empath gift can become a superpower if you are willing to put in the work – so let's get to it!

CHAPTER 10:

HOW TO DEVELOP YOUR CHAKRAS

Most people have heard about chakras as it's a common term used in yoga and meditation. But as an empath, you may be unaware of how important they are to your overall health and wellbeing, and your ability to operate in the fullness of your gift. To help you get started on enhancing your empath gift, this information will give you a massive head start.

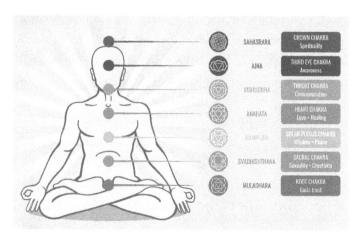

The book *Chakra Healing,* by Margarita Alcantara, states that the word "chakra" originates from the Sanskrit language and means "disk" or "wheel." Your energy is stored in the chakras, and like a wheel or a disk, and they are constantly spinning. Chakras must remain balanced or open to function at their best; if not, you are at risk of suffering from a chakra-related ailment. It is believed that the body is made up of at least 114 different chakras. Space constraints won't allow me to cover all of them, so I would advise that you do some additional research, but there are seven main chakras you definitely need to know about:

Crown Chakra: You will also hear the crown chakra referred to as the Sahasrara; it is positioned at the top of your head. The crown chakra determines how spiritually connected you are to the universe, yourself, and others. It is also related to your life's purpose.

Throat Chakra: The throat chakra is also called the Vishuddha, and it is found in the throat. It plays a role in verbal communication.

Heart Chakra: Also known as the Anahata, it is positioned in the center of the chest near your heart. The heart chakra determines our ability to show compassion and to love others.

Solar Plexus Chakra: Also referred to as the Manipura, the solar plexus chakra is found in the stomach area. It plays a role in self-esteem and confidence. It also gives you a sense of having control over your life.

Sacral Chakra: The sacral chakra is also known as Svadhisthana; you will find it right underneath the belly button. It is responsible for your creative and sexual energy. It also plays a role in how you connect with your emotions and the emotions of others.

Root Chakra: The root chakra is also called the Muladhara; you will find it at the base of the spine, and it provides you with a solid foundation for you to build your life on. When it is strong, you can withstand challenges, and it helps you feel grounded. Your root chakra plays a role in how stable and secure you feel in life.

Third Eye Chakra: Another name for the third eye chakra is Ajna. It is positioned between your eyes. When you get a "gut instinct," the third eye chakra is where it comes from. It plays a powerful role in intuition and imagination.

What Happens When Your Chakras Are Blocked?

According to yoga medicine therapeutic specialist Diane Malaspina, when the chakras are not working to their full potential, there is either too much energetic flow, or there is not enough energy flowing. Depending on where the blockage is, you will find it difficult to leverage the qualities linked to that chakra. An overactive chakra leads to those qualities becoming a dominant force in a person's life. For example, an underactive root chakra, which plays a role in stability and security, might manifest as insecurity and depression. If the root chakra is overactive, that person may take dangerous risks because they are fearless, or they might hoard things because having loads of stuff makes them feel secure.

A blocked chakra will typically affect the part of the body that it's in closest proximity to. Imbalances can also lead to emotional disturbances such as excessive fear, sadness, or indecisiveness. Guadalupe Terrones, a master reiki healer and certified yoga teacher, states that it's important to pay attention to the physical and psychological manifestations of chakra imbalances. There are many reasons why a chakra might get blocked, such as a bad diet, addictions, and even bad posture.

HOW TO UNBLOCK YOUR CHAKRAS

There are several ways to unblock chakras including meditation, breathing exercises, and yoga postures. However, as yoga is one of the most effective practices, it will be the focus in this section.

Tree Pose: This standing balancing pose works well for the root chakra because it helps build a stronger relationship with your body's foundation.

- Stand in a comfortable position and slowly lift your right foot upwards.

- Turn your foot inwards so the sole of your foot is resting against your left inner knee or thigh, depending on how high you can lift your leg.
- Do not press your foot into your leg.
- You can either keep your hands by your sides or bring them into a prayer position.
- Keep this pose for 2 minutes and then repeat on the opposite leg.

Bridge Pose: This yoga pose will unblock the sacral chakra and works to strengthen the pelvic floor muscles.

- Lie on your back and bend your knees, draw your heels into your sitting bone.
- Keep your arms flat on the floor by your side.
- Lift your tailbone upwards by pressing your arms and feet into the floor.
- Keep lifting your thighs upwards until they are parallel to the floor.
- Support yourself by placing your hands under your hips.
- Remain in the pose for 1 minute.
- To come out of the pose, roll your spine down slowly.
- Fold your knees in together.
- Breathe deeply and relax in this position.

The Triangle Pose: The triangle pose works to unblock the solar plexus chakra by strengthening the core.

- Stand and position your feet so they are wider than your hips.
- Position your right toes at an angle, and your left toes facing forward.
- With your palms facing downwards, stretch your arms out on either side of you.
- With your left hand, reach forward and extend the top half of your body forward.
- Push your right hip back and touch your left leg with your left hand.
- Point your right arm up toward the ceiling.
- Keep the pose for one minute and then do the same on the other side.

Cow Face Pose: To unblock the heart chakra yoga, experts recommend the cow face pose.

- Take a deep breath in and, with your palm facing downwards, stretch out your right arm.
- Put your arm behind your back and reach up to touch your shoulder blades.
- Lift your left arm upwards, and grab hold of your right hand.
- Gently pull your right hand upwards.
- Hold the pose for one minute and then repeat on the other side.

The Plow Pose: The plow pose is good for the throat chakra, and it works by increasing circulation, stimulating the thyroid gland, and reducing stress.

- Lie on your back and raise your legs above your head so they touch the floor behind you.
- Support yourself by keeping your hands on your lower back.
- Keep the pose for 1 to 5 minutes.
- Slowly release yourself from the pose.

The Forward Fold: This pose is used to unblock the third eye chakra.

- Stand straight and take a deep breath in at the same time as stretching your arms out to the sides and lifting them over your head.
- Breathe out at the same time as stretching your arms forward and folding your torso over so your head is touching your knees and your arms are folded around your calves.
- Remain in this position for one minute.

Corpse Pose: The corpse pose is used to unblock the crown chakra. Because of its resting position, it is used as a reward pose after a yoga workout.

- Lie on your back with your legs outstretched and your arms to the sides but not touching your body.
- Keep your palms facing upwards.

- Remain in this pose for as long as you need to.
- Now that you've unblocked your chakras, you are free to start operating in the fullness of your empath gift.

CHAPTER 11:

HOW TO MANAGE YOUR NEGATIVE EMOTIONS

Due to the intensity with which empaths feel things, it is essential that they manage their negative emotions the right way or they can spin out of control. But managing negative emotions doesn't mean avoiding them. Many people cope with the emotions they don't want to feel by avoiding them, and this can do more harm than good. Managing negative emotions is about embracing

them, understanding why we are feeling them, releasing them, and moving forward. Here are some tips to help you manage your negative emotions:

Calm Down: The body reacts to emotions; they are a type of stimulation. For example, when you are afraid, your muscles get tense and your heart starts beating faster. When you are angry, you think about the incident that made you angry. When you are nervous or anxious, your mind races with thoughts about the unknown. By calming down, the impact of the emotion felt is weakened. Slow, deep breathing is the fastest way to calm down, because as mentioned, the pace of breath speeds up during an emotional meltdown. Try taking slow, deep breaths the next time you feel overwhelmed, and pay attention to the way it makes you feel.

Relax Tense Muscles: When the muscles tense up, it signals to the brain that something is wrong, and it triggers the release of stress hormones such as cortisol. Relax your muscles by going for a walk or moving your body. At the same time, shift your thinking to something positive like a good memory or a peaceful location. Once you change your thoughts, your actions will follow.

Process It: When bad feelings come up, most people don't want to deal with them and will suppress them instead. Fake it until you make it, but don't neglect to process the emotion. As discussed in chapter 5, emotions are designed to move through the body, and when negative emotions are left unresolved, they get stuck and manifest as sickness and disease. Therefore, take some time out to process the emotion, think about it, and work out why you are feeling this way. Additionally, by thinking about it, you might come up with a solution to the problem, which will make you feel better.

Express It: Now, this is not a free pass to go and cause someone physical harm. You might be really angry and feel like slapping someone. But instead of lashing out, release the emotion by lifting weights or going for a run. If you are the creative type, negative emotions often motivate people to operate in their talent. If you are feeling sad, you might be inspired to write a poem. Some of the world's best-loved music was written when the writer was experiencing an extreme emotion. For example, Chris from Coldplay wrote the song "Fix You" after his wife's father died. Another way of releasing negative emotions is to talk about what's bothering you to someone you trust. Basically, do whatever you need to do to release negative emotions.

Change Your Perspective: Not everything is the way it seems. When you have encountered a setback or something hasn't turned out the way you had planned, negative thoughts can take over and you end up stuck in that frame of mind. Let's say you've lost your job; the first thing you think is, "How am I going to pay my bills?" This thought will turn into, "I am going to get kicked out of my apartment", this thought turns into, "I'm going to end up on the streets." There are all sorts of directions your negative thoughts can take you in. But if you are going to manage your emotions, you must change your perspective when you are facing a bad situation. Yes, losing your job is stressful, and fear is going to set in because you don't know how you are going to pay your bills. I am not saying these are not valid fears – have a pity party, just don't make it a big one. Pick yourself up and tell yourself that losing your job has cleared the way for you to get another job with more pay, or that you've now got the time to start your own business. Whatever negative situation you are facing, learn to look at it from a positive angle.

Focus on What's Important: What goals have you set for yourself? What date have you set for you to achieve those goals? That should be your main focus. The universe has a funny way of rewarding people who want to succeed in life, and the moment you set out to do something worthwhile, all hell breaks loose. Not to worry, you are just one in a sea of millions of people who this happens to, so you are not special. Challenges, distractions, and frustrations are designed to pull you away from your purpose, but you've got to make a conscious decision not to allow them to derail you. If all your energy and attention is directed towards anything other than your main goal, guess what? You will never achieve it. And a lack of achievement will lower your self-esteem and make you feel terrible about yourself. Conversely, when you are working toward your goals and seeing progress, you feel energized and fulfilled.

Imagine Your Ideal Self: We all have an ideal self because everyone desires to make improvements in their life. One of the reasons people give in to their negative emotions and become depressed is because they are not happy with who they've become. They have their ideal self in the back of their mind, but then wake up to the cruel reality of the person staring back at them in the mirror every day. When you feel down, think about this person; start by writing down exactly who you want to become and the life you want to live. Spend time meditating on that person and visualizing it; get all your five senses involved, smell the sweet aromas coming from your fancy restaurant. See the magnificent penthouse view overlooking the ocean. If you want children, hear the sounds of happy laughter abounding through your home. Imagine how that silk pillowcase feels when you rest your head on it at night.

Research suggests that performing this exercise for five minutes each day makes you feel a lot more optimistic about life and helps to improve your mood when you are feeling low. Imagining your best self is great, but taking massive action to get there is even better.

Take the Day Off: Whether it's once a month or once a week, take a day off and do whatever makes you happy. Taking the day off provides a much-needed interruption to the stresses of life, because whether we want it to be or not, life is stressful. There is always something waiting to weigh us down. But when you are well-rested and you feel content, you will have the strength you need to effectively deal with the challenges that come your way.

Fake It Until You Make It: The body communicates what it's feeling to the brain, and based on that information, an emotional response is created, and the brain will release a hormone that supports that emotion. For example, if you are feeling sad but smile for three minutes, your brain will think you are happy and will release endorphins to support your corresponding emotion. Let's say you are going for a job interview and you are feeling nervous; make a power pose by standing with your hands on your hips and your feet shoulder-width apart. The pose will make you feel more self-assured. When your behavior reflects the emotion you desire, you will start to feel it.

One of the consequences of suppressing negative emotions or allowing them to become overwhelming is anxiety. We will deal with this in the next chapter.

CHAPTER 12:

HOW TO DEAL WITH ANXIETY

Whether it's because of a household move, school exams, or going through a divorce, everyone experiences anxiety at some point in their life. However, it becomes a problem when those feelings remain for extended periods, or never go away. Empaths spend a lot of time in a state of anxiety, whether it's as a result of their feelings or someone else's. A study published in the *Journal of Psychiatry* found that people who suffer from social phobia are attentive and sensitive to the states of mind of

others. It's not always easy to speak about anxiety, especially for empaths, when there is nothing causing it other than the fact that they've picked up on someone else's energy. In some cases, you might not even be aware that it's anxiety you are feeling. To start, here are some signs that you are experiencing anxiety:

- Feeling shaky and weak
- Muscle tension
- Sweating, nausea, trembling, shallow breathing, a racing heart
- Self-medicating by overeating or consuming alcohol
- Collecting/hoarding
- Being overly concerned with safety
- Becoming obsessed with routine
- Becoming unwilling to take part in normal activities
- Excessive worry or fear
- Indigestion
- Diarrhea
- Irritable bowel syndrome
- Frequent urination
- Dry mouth
- Blurred vision

You can probably relate to some of the signs mentioned above because you've either experienced them before or you are going through them now. Additionally, there are several types of anxiety and it's important to have a brief understanding of what they are:

Generalized Anxiety Disorder (GAD): GAD is the most common form of anxiety, and it occurs when people feel overwhelmed about anything and everything including health, money, possible disasters, family problems, etc.

Obsessive-Compulsive Disorder (OCD): Obsessive-compulsive disorder is present when a person suffers from repeated unwanted images and thoughts. They feel a deep need to perform certain actions such as washing their hands all the time, turning on all the lights, doing things in a certain order, touching certain things all the time, or hoarding items that are not needed.

Panic Disorder: This type of anxiety involves experiencing sudden attacks of terror which come in the form of nausea, dizziness, faintness, weakness, sweatiness, chest pain, or pounding heart. These attacks can happen at any time, and they typically last for around 10 minutes, but sometimes these symptoms can last longer. It is not uncommon for people experiencing a panic attack to think they are having a stroke.

A Phobia: This form of anxiety is an extreme fear of an object, an animal, a situation, or a place. Social anxiety or social phobia is a common phobia; those who suffer from this condition feel extremely self-conscious and anxious in normal everyday situations such as going to the store.

Agoraphobia: This anxiety involves being afraid of going to places where it would be difficult to escape.

Claustrophobia: A fear of enclosed spaces.

As a person who carries the energy of others, you could experience any one of these forms of anxiety at any given moment. For example, if you are in a room with someone who is claustrophobic, you might suddenly start feeling frightened and not understand why.

NEGATIVE THINKING PATTERNS

No one is immune to negative thinking, and even those who don't suffer from anxiety sometimes struggle with thinking the worst. The main difference between negative thinking and negative thinking patterns is that a pattern is not an occasional negative thought, but a fixed and habitual way of thinking that drives behavior. Here are some negative thinking patterns to be aware of:

- **Commanding the Self:** Perfectionists are prone to think in this way. They give themselves rigid deadlines and instructions and don't take into account the fact that sometimes, circumstances can change.

- **Self-Blame:** Self-blame is when every situation is viewed through a negative lens. For example, you post something on social media and the people you are expecting to comment or like your content don't respond. As a result, you immediately jump to the conclusion that they didn't engage with your post because they are tired of seeing your pictures in their feed, or that they don't like you. Meanwhile, the reality is that there were different reasons why no one commented on your post ranging from they didn't check their account that day, to your post didn't show up in their feed, or they saw the post and got distracted with something else and forgot to come back to it.

- **Over-Generalizing:** An example of over-generalizing includes getting your heart broken by a man which leads you to conclude that all men are dogs. Because of one bad experience, you make the decision that you are never going to get married. Or you are a writer, and someone gives you a 2-star review; therefore, you decide that you must be a terrible writer and make the decision never to write another book.

- **All or Nothing/Black or White Thinking:** Life is full of colors, and no situation is ever as it seems. All or nothing thinking is an extreme way of processing information that stops you from thinking outside the box. For example, you've just lost your job and so now you have convinced yourself that your life is over. You use absolute terms such as "never," or "ever" and you are incapable of seeing the positive side of losing your job such as, you've now got the time to work on your dreams, or you can start looking for a higher paid or more enjoyable or convenient job.

People with negative thinking patterns believe the glass is always half-empty, so it is a pessimistic way of being that leads to a destructive view of life. Someone with an anxiety disorder will have one bad day which causes them to think that every day of their life is going to be bad. Thoughts are powerful and we attract what we think. Someone who is always thinking the worst will experience the worst, which then provides them with the evidence required to justify the way they think. And thus, the downward spiral begins.

HOW TO CHALLENGE NEGATIVE THINKING

Negative thinking is intimidating and frightening, especially when we don't believe we have any control over it. But once you understand how you can challenge those thoughts, you can redirect them and change the pattern of negative thinking. Here are some tips on how to do so:

- **Recognize the Thought Loop:** Start by paying attention to the way you think; are you an all-or-nothing thinker? Or a self-blame thinker? Additionally, negative thinking is often triggered by something that encourages the thought loop. What is it that incites these reactions? Are there things in your environment that contribute to it? If so, eliminate them. It may even be the case that there are friends and family members in your life who encourage negative thinking. If so, distance yourself from them. Do you find that this thought pattern starts when you watch distressing programs on TV?

If so, stop watching them. Nevertheless, when you remove these things, you will need to replace them with something positive. So, instead of spending the night speaking to negative Nancy, spend the evening listening to a motivational speaker.

- **Question Your Thinking:** When it comes to politics and you are deciding who to vote for, you don't take what they say at face value. To decide whether they are telling the truth, you question what they are saying. You can question your own thinking in the same way; when you find yourself traveling down that slippery slope of negative thinking, instead of running with those thoughts, question why you are thinking that way. First, what happened that has caused you to start thinking like this? Second, is your reaction justified? And third, what other ways can you think about this situation? Questioning your emotions in this way will help you get to the root of the problem.

- **Pay Attention to Something Else:** Negative thinking can overwhelm you and send you on a downward spiral of decline. One negative thought leads to another, and then another and before you know it, you are stuck. Before, you get to this point, interrupt those thoughts by paying attention to something else. Going for a run, reading a few pages of a book out loud, or listening to uplifting music are just a few ways you can distract yourself. These a just a handful of suggestions and we are all different, so do whatever makes you feel comfortable.

- **Replace the Negative Thought:** Instead of thinking about what you don't have, focus on what you do have. Let's say you are not happy with your weight, and all you keep thinking about is how terrible you look in your clothes. Instead of focusing on your weight, think about how grateful you are to have a roof over your head, a job to pay the bills, and loving friends and family to support you on your weight loss journey. Even if it is true that you are unhappy with your weight, start working on it. But while you are taking steps to lose weight, remind yourself that there are things in your life you are grateful for, and the more action you take, the sooner you will arrive at your ideal weight.

- **Stop Being Judgmental:** This refers to judging yourself, not other people. Anxious people give themselves a hard time by constantly comparing themselves to the unhealthy standards of society. We are indirectly told that if you haven't got the mansion, the perfect looking partner, 2.4 children, and the vacation home on a luxury island by the age of 35, then you've failed in life. It is easy to buy into these standards and use them as a yardstick by which to judge yourself, especially when you are constantly looking for evidence to confirm your inner negative voice. If buying magazines, scrolling through social media, and watching TV make you feel insecure, stop giving them your energy. Instead, use that time to focus on bettering yourself and becoming your own version of perfect.

- **Practice Gratitude:** Do you remember the last time you got a surprise that you were grateful for? Maybe it was your birthday and you got the present you wanted, or your partner surprised you with a romantic dinner one night after work. You actually felt something deep inside, and at that moment, you felt happy and content. The aim of practicing gratitude is to get you into that emotional state every day. It is something you should embrace as soon as you wake up in the morning, and before you go to bed at night. Follow these steps to practice gratitude:

  - Buy a journal and label it your gratitude journal.
  - Write down five things in your life that you are grateful for.
  - Focus on those things and feel the emotion of gratitude.
  - Keep your mind on that feeling for ten minutes.
  - Leave the journal on your bedside table so you don't forget.
  - You can also practice gratitude during the day when you start thinking negative thoughts.

HOW TO PROTECT YOURSELF AGAINST ANXIETY

Anxiety is not a nice feeling, and it's one of the many negative emotions that empaths are forced to deal with. The good news is there are things you can do to protect yourself against anxiety.

Exercise: Outside of keeping fit and healthy, there are many reasons why you should exercise, and managing anxiety is one of them. Please note, if you are new to exercising, don't rush into it, start slowly and be sensible. It feels good thinking about the weights you are going to lift at the gym, but you don't want to injure yourself. To begin, a brisk walk or a light jog will be enough.

Additionally, you can play a sport or take part in a hobby you enjoy such as dancing or gardening. The idea is to get your body moving. As mentioned, start slowly and work your way up to 20-40 minutes three to four times per week. Here are some of the benefits of exercise:

- Helps the body get rid of stress hormones
- Burns excess tension and energy from the muscles
- Improves your breathing pattern
- Releases endorphins which are a natural anti-depressant
- Reduces feelings of anger, frustration, and tension
- Improves the immune system
- Improves sleep
- Distracts you from worry

Breathing: Until you can't breathe, breathing is not something you think about. However, it plays an important role in how the nervous system works; therefore, it makes sense that we should learn to breathe in a way that will ensure the body works the way it is supposed to. When we breathe in the right way, it has a positive effect on the biochemical reactions in the body which have physical and mental effects on us. Research suggests that people who suffer from anxiety disorders are shallow breathers; they breathe through their chest, and chest breathing has a negative effect on the balance of oxygen and carbon dioxide, which is required to maintain a healthy, relaxed state.

By taking deep breaths and breathing slowly, adrenaline is reduced because the heart rate slows down. Make proper breathing a daily habit by performing the following exercises:

- **Belly Breathing:** Belly breathing works well when you are having a panic attack. It helps reduce the excessive breathing that results from hyperventilating. Regardless of your stress levels, belly breathing will help you take control of the physical discomfort associated with anxiety.

  - Sit or stand in a relaxed position with your shoulders down.
  - To feel how you are breathing, place one hand on your chest, the other on your stomach.
  - Take a slow, deep breath in through your nose. Your chest will rise, and your stomach will expand.

- Slightly purse your lips, keeping your jaw and tongue relaxed, and breathe out through your mouth. You will hear a slight whistling sound.
- The key to relaxation is the exhale, so make this as long and as smooth as possible.
- Repeat this exercise for 10 minutes.

- **The Measured Breath:** A popular breathing technique that helps reduce feelings of anxiety:

  - Stand or sit and relax your body.
  - Relax your jaw and drop your shoulders.
  - Slowly take a deep breath through your nose while counting to four.
  - Your stomach should expand while you breathe in.
  - After breathing all the way in, hold your breath for four seconds.
  - At the same time as counting to seven, breath out smoothly and slowly.
  - Repeat the exercise for ten minutes.

Bumble Bee Breathing: This is not the best breathing exercise to perform if you are prone to feeling anxious in public because it requires that you make a bit of noise. Bumble bee breathing is a very popular breathing technique that has been used for thousands of years to help calm the mind:

- Sit or stand in a comfortable position and relax your shoulders.

- Restrict your throat so you can hear yourself when you breathe.
- Cover your eyes with your fingers and cover your ears with your thumbs.
- Lightly close your lips and lightly put your teeth together.
- Relax your jaw and slowly breathe out, making a low humming sound.
- Repeat this 5 to 10 times and then relax by taking deep breaths.

CHANGE THE WAY YOU THINK

People who suffer from anxiety tend to have very negative thinking patterns. Your thoughts influence the way you feel, so if you can control the way you think, it will assist in relieving feelings of overwhelm. Common thoughts associated with anxiety include:

- Always thinking that something bad is going to happen
- Obsessed with getting to a place of safety
- Being unable to concentrate
- Intrusive, obsessive thoughts
- Feeling disconnected from others
- A blank mind
- Forgetfulness
- Confusion
- Self-critical thoughts
- Increased sensitivity to criticism

Anxious people are very self-critical and will tell themselves they are useless and failures. These thoughts can create feelings such as:

- Sadness
- Loneliness
- Apathy
- Anger
- Shame
- Guilt
- Worry
- Impatience
- Frustration
- Terror
- Nervousness

Negative thinking is the catalyst for anxiety which causes a vicious cycle that is difficult to break out of. Nevertheless, it is more than possible to change the way you think; you control your thoughts, your thoughts don't control you. You have the power to influence your thoughts by challenging the way you think. Once you gain control of your thoughts, your mood will improve, and the anxiety will dissipate.

Anxious people think in patterns of black and white. They polarize their thinking and will either see themselves as terrible failures or, on a good day, massively successful. It's basically all or nothing. An anxious person will wake up in the morning and their first thought will sound something like, "My day is already ruined because I'm going to feel anxious all day." But you can change this narrative by thinking something like, "There is a chance that I could have a good day." There is an alternative to the worst-case scenario; once you put this into practice, you will find that you don't have to think negatively all the time, because sometimes life isn't that bad after all.

Handling Criticism: There are two types of criticism, constructive criticism, which is when the person doing the criticism is trying to get you to improve in a certain area of your life. Then there are people who just criticize because they are being nasty. No one likes being told they are not good enough, especially when deep down, that is how they feel about themselves. However, anxious people don't like any form of criticism because it confirms their negative inner voice. But when it comes to handling criticism, it's important to understand two things; first, you need to know the difference between constructive criticism and destructive criticism. Second, it's impossible to please everyone, and so some people are not going to like you, no matter what you do.

Constructive criticism will often come from a friend, family member, or co-worker who has spotted a weakness in you and has a genuine desire for you to improve in that area. Very few people acknowledge their weaknesses and make a conscious decision to make changes. For some of us, it's just too much work, but if you want to become the best version of yourself, learning what your weaknesses are and doing everything you can to strengthen yourself in those areas is a good idea.

When people criticize you for no reason, it's important to understand that you can't change the opinions of others. Think about it like this; the best chef in the world can cook a meal for 10 people – seven of those people are blown away by the food, and the other three are horrified. They all write a review about the meal and the three who didn't like it say some terrible things (not because they are being rude, but that's how they genuinely feel). The other seven write brilliant reviews. Turns out, the three people who wrote negative reviews did so because they hate the herb oregano, and since they don't like the herb, they are sensitive to it. The other seven love oregano and mention how satisfying the oregano flavor was. Now the chef can either read the negative reviews and get offended, or he can look at it from a different perspective which might be, "There was no way I could have known that they didn't like oregano," or "Seven good reviews out of ten is a win for me."

The anxious person will find this response difficult to embrace because of their polarized thinking. One bad review will lead them to keep rehearsing the narrative in their head that they are a bad chef, when the reality is, it's impossible to please everyone. When you understand that criticism is based on someone's opinion and that it is not confirmation of who you are as a person, it makes criticism easier to endure. The next time you feel the sting of a critical remark remind yourself of the following:

- It is rare that things are either just good or just bad.
- The truth can fall anywhere between 0 and 100%.

- Consider whether there is anything you can learn from the criticism.
- If the criticism is of no use, let it go.

Tip: Keep a box with all your cards in it, the ones on which friends, family members, and coworkers have written nice things about you. Whenever you get anxious and can't stop thinking negative thoughts about yourself, read those cards to remind yourself there are plenty of people who think you are awesome.

Perfectionism: Perfectionists typically have a very loud negative inner voice that is constantly screaming to their soul about how terrible they are. Anxious people are obsessed with getting everything right and will convince themselves that it's a strength. Unfortunately, perfectionism can become a serious hindrance when the slightest thing that goes wrong is seen as the biggest failure in the world.

The problem is that people who want to be perfect are terrified of making mistakes, and this can either cause procrastination, where a person never gets started because of fear, or they agonize over small details and become obsessed with improving and checking. Since so much time and effort was spent working on the project, if they don't get good feedback all around, the harsh inner voice starts with the negative self-talk. Therefore, perfectionism can have a negative effect on your mental health because sometimes, you are either going to get it wrong, or whatever you are doing is not going to be perfect. Think about it like this: even the greatest performers in the world don't win all the time. Denzel Washington doesn't always get an Oscar, Cristiano Ronaldo doesn't always score the winning goal and Justin Bieber doesn't always win a Grammy. Perfectionism isn't a requirement for success because every successful person has a story of failure to tell. Consistency and determination are much more important than perfectionism. Here are some tips on practicing being imperfect:

- Instead of spending the entire day cleaning, give yourself 20 minutes for each room. Get as much done as possible during that time and then move on to the next room.
- If you need to write a report for work or an essay for school, depending on the length, give yourself a small timeframe to complete it instead of spending the hours that you usually would on it.
- Reward yourself for underachievement.

Your anxiety isn't going to disappear overnight, but as you put these strategies into practice, you will learn to quickly shut down anxiety when it arises.

CHAPTER 13:

HOW TO CONTROL YOUR ENERGY

We live in a metaphysical world in which everything is energy, even the device you are holding to read this book. The human body is fueled by energy from the foods we eat and without it, we can't function. The energy we run on is like electricity: it powers us, but we can't see it. Empaths understand this more than others because they are so sensitive to energy. Some empaths can see the energy that radiates from a person's body, while others can sense it. The empath knows that with every interaction,

there is an exchange of energy. Because empaths have a higher sense of perception, they know and feel things about people on a more intimate level. Nevertheless, when an empath doesn't know how to control their energy, they get overwhelmed and the gift becomes a burden. To operate at your full potential, one of the things you must learn to do is control your energy.

Shielding Visualization: Shielding through visualization is a powerful technique that allows you to protect your energy field instantly, no matter where you are. Although it takes quite a bit of practice to master, once you've got it, it is really easy to turn on and off. Additionally, you will gain full control of your body and what you allow into your energy field. Here are the steps for the shielding visualization:

- Imagine that everyone's body is surrounded by a force field. Give the force field a name and a color. The color can be the same for each person or different.
- Some ideas for a force field include flowing water, a glowing light, or a cloud.
- Visualize the field as an extension of their body; like an item of clothing, it is surrounding them.
- Visualize the same force field around yourself.
- See the force field around yourself moving like fog, water, or light.
- Your force field fits differently from everyone else's because it hangs more loosely. It moves in the wind and travels wherever it wants.

- Visualize your force field gravitating towards the people around you like metal to a magnet.
- It flows towards them like a river and gets caught up in their force field.
- Visualize the force field floating back to you; it contains pieces of the other person's force field in it.
- Your force field comes back to you containing the force field of the other people and it attaches itself to you.
- Now imagine that your force field is under your full control.
- Pull your force field in towards you and away from the other people in the room.
- Wrap your force field around your body and secure it in any way you choose, such as by sewing it or harnessing it.
- Your force field wants to drift away, but don't allow it to. Visualize it remaining on you.
- Notice that it is still covered in the stuff from the other people.
- Visualize yourself shaking it off like you are removing dust from an old rug.
- Watch as the energy that doesn't belong to you falls to the ground.
- Visualize your force field going from cloudy and muddled to free and pure.
- Watch as it shines and glistens because it no longer contains energy that doesn't belong to you.

- As you put your force field back on, feel how lightweight it is and how much easier it is to carry around now that all that baggage has been removed.
- Each time your force field starts traveling in the direction of other people, remind yourself that absorbing other people's energy is of no benefit to you. It weighs you down and makes you feel drained and tired so that you don't have anything to give to the people who really need it.

One final word of advice… it takes practice and mindfulness to master this visualization. Spend some time meditating on it and get familiar with the mental image so you can easily call it to mind when you are trapped in a situation with energy vampires. If you believe you have the power to control what enters your emotional space, you will achieve it.

SET THE TONE IN YOUR RELATIONSHIPS

Empaths have a hard time in relationships for several reasons, and one of the most detrimental is that they feel responsible for their partner's happiness. They want to fix every broken part of them and as a result, it is not uncommon for empaths to attract the wrong people (such as narcissists), or to overstay in their relationships. The downfall of many empaths is their relationships, in which they end up trapped and depressed and they never flourish in their gift. That's why I think empaths should master their gift before getting into a relationship. You can compare this to someone who dates when they don't love themselves and they are looking for someone to fill the void. Sadly, people like this end up in abusive relationships because they are willing to settle for less, just for the sake of having someone in their lives. When empaths haven't mastered their gift, it becomes very easy for them to lose touch with who they really are. Nevertheless, you can protect your energy by setting the tone in your relationships.

You Are Not Responsible for Their Emotions: You must keep this at the forefront of your mind at all times or you will get sucked into every aspect of your partner's well-being. Some people don't process their emotions well, so you could end up dating someone who bottles things up all the time. He does this because as a child, he was forbidden from expressing his emotions in the home. As a result, he has a negative view of emotions such as anger, frustration, and hurt. When something is wrong, instead of speaking about it, he/she will shut down. Since you can feel emotions and know something isn't right, you spend your time and energy trying to get them to open up, but nothing seems to work. In the meantime, you are getting sick, depressed, and depleted, because whether intentionally, or unintentionally, your partner is draining the life out of you. You must go into your relationships with a fixed mindset that says you are not going to carry your partner's emotions because they don't belong to you.

Own Your Personal Power: Whether you're male or female, it's important that you own your personal power when you are in a relationship. This is not about wearing the pants and dominating the other person, but about being assertive. All relationships are about compromise, but if you feel that you are compromising your overall happiness, then you might need to reconsider whether this is the right person for you. When you don't agree with something, let your partner know. If you feel more comfortable having a separate bank account, articulate this. Never remain silent because you are afraid of hurting your partner's feelings. Empaths are good at giving their power away because they don't like upsetting the status quo, they despise confrontation, and so tend to tolerate things that they shouldn't.

Become a Spectator: Keep yourself physically energized, energetically centered, and emotionally balanced by becoming an observer of your partner instead of sharing in their feelings. When the average person is around an upset person, they will go above and beyond to comfort the person, but they are observing those feelings because they don't really know how they feel. An empath, however, feels exactly what the other person feels and ends up carrying those emotions long after they have left the company of that individual. Because empaths are so emotional, they tend to react first and think about it later. If you are going to effectively set the tone in your relationships, you must become intentional about becoming a spectator. Train your mind to think before you get absorbed in the feeling. When an empath feels something, they get lost in the feeling and they find it difficult to bring themselves back. Training your mind not to get absorbed in your feelings takes practice, but it's possible. Follow these steps to get started:

- When you feel an emotion, immediately stop whatever you are doing and think about why you are feeling it.
- Ask yourself whether the emotion belongs to you.
- When you realize that the emotion doesn't belong to you, give it back to that person by speaking it out. You may need to go into another room to do this; you can say something like, "I denounce these emotions, I am returning them to the person they came from."
- Keep saying this until you feel a release. Once the emotion has left you, begin spectating.

Demand Your Physical Space: It is only natural that people need their space in a relationship, but empaths need this space more than the average person. It is not uncommon for people with empath partners to complain about the amount of alone time they need. Empaths need space to release negative energy and recharge their batteries. If possible, dedicate a spare room in the house for this, and ensure no one goes into that room but you, so the positive energy you leave in there remains. Additionally, empaths need to live in a clutter-free and clean environment. Empaths are often minimalists; they feel very uncomfortable when there's a lot of stuff around. Having a messy partner can be particularly distressing to an empath; if this is the case, you will need to put your foot down and let them know in no uncertain terms that you cannot tolerate mess in your living space.

Avoid People-Pleasing: Empaths people-please because they want everyone to be happy and they don't want to deal with confrontation. But life doesn't work like that; as much as empaths want to live in a perfect world, it will never happen. There is always going to be conflict because it's impossible for everyone to agree all the time. The irony is that people-pleasing might help to maintain the status quo externally, but the empath ends up internalizing their frustration, which is another issue in itself. If you experience any of the following, you are people-pleasing:

- You compromise your boundaries even if your partner doesn't try to.
- You stop expressing your needs, which leads to you feeling neglected and unloved.
- You become so focused on your partner that you fail to take care of yourself.
- You deal with things internally; you will have an argument in your head so you don't have it with your partner.

Now that you know you are people-pleasing, it's time to stop. Here are some tips on how you can do this:

- **Think Before You Agree:** When your partner asks you for a favor, think about whether that favor is going to inconvenience you. As mentioned, it is important to compromise when you are in a relationship, but if you are going to be so inconvenienced that it causes you distress, don't do it.

- **Create a Mantra:** When you realize you've stepped into people-pleasing mode, say your mantra. It might be something like, "I have freed myself from people-pleasing."

- **Empathic Assertion:** Empaths should be good at this because they really do know how people feel. Nevertheless, the difficulty for an empath is that it requires being assertive. Empathic assertion dictates that when a person asks you to do something that you are unable to, you should explain that you understand where they are coming from, but that it's not possible. Here is an example: "I appreciate that you need someone to take you to the doctor's office today, but this is not a valid reason to take leave, and if I do, I won't get paid for the time." The person might then ask you to lie so you can get paid and still take the day off. You can then respond with, "I understand how much you need someone to be there for you during this procedure, however, I do not feel comfortable lying to my boss." It is also advised that you don't use the same phrases. You will notice that I went from saying, "I appreciate," to "I understand," because when you keep repeating the same thing, you don't sound sincere; it's almost as if you are being sarcastic. So, don't forget to switch it up a bit.

Remove Yourself from the Environment: Empaths love connecting with people, but they also need to spend a lot of time alone to get a break from absorbing other people's emotions and reconnect with their own. Therefore, it is not uncommon for empaths to be mistaken for introverts. Without alone time, it is easy to crumble under pressure; on the other hand, you need to maintain healthy relationships for the sake of your mental health. Empaths often struggle with this dichotomy because as soon as they step outside the house, they are hit with whatever emotions are lingering in their environment. Some empaths deal with this by going to chill places like a friend's house or a coffee shop instead of parties and nightclubs. Nevertheless, even being in a relaxed location can lead to overwhelm; for example, you might go to a friend's house and her depressed mother comes to visit. Before she has even stepped into the same room you can feel her energy. When you shake her hand, the tension gets even worse. When you find yourself in a situation like this, remove yourself from the environment; go outside for a few minutes. If that doesn't work, tell your friend that something's come up and you've got to go home. You can call your friend later to explain; your closest friends will know that you're an empath, and they will understand.

If you are stuck in a location and it's not possible to leave, stay as far away as possible from the offending party. Empaths are so sensitive to energy that they can sense the direction it's coming from. So if you are in a room full of people and you feel negative energy coming from the left, move further to the right and vice versa.

As an empath, you must protect your energy at all costs, it's like the fuel to your fire. Without good energy, you become powerless, and you were not created to be powerless. You are a magnificently powerful being who has the ability to achieve some amazing feats in the world.

CHAPTER 14:

THE MOST EFFECTIVE GROUNDING TECHNIQUES

t is not uncommon to hear empaths describe, "feeling floaty, with no anchor" or "so light, you could blow at me and I would fall over." This sounds like an ideal state to be in… after all, who doesn't want to feel like they are rising above the problems of life? The issue is that when empaths feel this way, they hit rock bottom very quickly because they feel overwhelmed with chaotic energy. When empaths

are earthed, they feel supported and calm. Here are a few reasons why grounding is important to empaths:

- Grounding provides a landing point for their life's purpose.
- Grounding improves empathic, emotional, and mental clarity.
- Grounding brings an instant feeling of calm.
- Grounding rejuvenates and restores our energy field.
- Grounding provides energetic support.
- Grounding provides an immediate solution for getting rid of unwanted energy.

Additionally, grounding is about getting rid of trapped negative energy. Positive emotions make us feel light and fluffy, they make us want to smile, dance, run, or sing. Negative emotions also cause a reaction in the body such as an increase in blood pressure, muscle contractions, and slumped shoulders. When these negative emotions get stuck in the tissues, they can cause sickness in the body. This is one of the reasons why empaths get sick a lot. Emotions are not designed to remain in the body but to pass through it. When you find something funny, you laugh until you've released the desire to laugh. When you stub your toe against the corner of a desk, the pain might make you feel angry which causes you to curse or punch the air with your fists. These natural responses allow emotions to flow through and then out of the body. Isn't it interesting how positive emotions flow freely through the body, but negative emotions can get stuck? One of the main reasons for this is that people don't like to face negative emotions, which makes it easy to suppress them. This becomes even more complicated for empaths who don't understand their gift because they are not aware they are carrying the emotions of others. Empaths are prone to suppressing negative emotions as a protective mechanism. When an emotion can't make its natural path through the body because of resistance, it becomes locked in the tissues of the body, and after a while, it causes illness.

GROUNDING TECHNIQUES

There are so many effective grounding techniques that it would take a separate book to write about them all, so I am just going to give you a few of the most popular, and maybe you can look into some more techniques for yourself.

Wear a Crystal Necklace: Black tourmaline crystal protects the wearer against negative energy from other people. You should wear this necklace at all times because not only does it act as a barrier to negative energy, it sends it back where it came from. Additionally, here are six crystals all empaths should have:

- **Clear Quartz:** This is a universal healing stone that boosts the power of other stones so that when their energy is focused in a certain direction, it is stronger. In addition, clear quartz balances the crown chakra which strengthens the connection to a higher power.

- **Amethyst:** You will also hear the amethyst referred to as the sober stone because it helps addicts remain substance-free when they are in recovery. People also carry it when they are traveling because it acts as a form of protection while a person is making their way to their destination. Amethyst improves sleep, stimulates dreams, and strengthens your connection with your intuition. It supports the third eye chakra and eliminates psychological problems, eye issues, and migraines.

- **Celestite:** Celestite is a throat chakra crystal that improves communication, speaking your truth, and creative expression. It also relieves throat, thyroid, gum, jaw, teeth, and mouth issues.

- **Rose Quartz:** This crystal is a heart chakra stone that helps people release bitterness and anger. It also assists people who are struggling with forgiveness and compassion for others. Rose quartz keeps romantic and unconditional love flowing.

- **Citrine:** Citrine is a prosperity stone; it also helps with solar plexus issues, boosts self-esteem and strengthens willpower.

- **Carnelian:** This crystal works with the sacral chakra for finances, to work through problems with sexuality and to help people get a better understanding of their purpose in life.

Animals: A study conducted by the University of Helsinki discovered that empaths have stronger connections with dogs than with humans. You might not have a dog, but, in general, empaths love animals because they are so similar. They are naturally instinctive, and they are always in their natural state. Animals love people unconditionally and don't expect anything in return. If you have a pet, spending time with it is a powerful way to ground yourself because just like you, all animals want is love.

Have Fun: Having fun is one of the easiest ways to ground yourself because you are focusing on the present moment. One of the components of being grounded is staying present, and when you are having fun, your mind is centered on the activity at hand and not on the overwhelm you are experiencing. Everyone's definition of fun is different: it might involve jumping on a trampoline, singing, dancing, or watching a movie.

Stop Overeating: When empaths are not grounded, they overeat; the reason is that when they are full, they no longer experience that floaty feeling because they are heavy and feel weighed down to the ground. One of the consequences of eating too much is feeling lethargic and sick, which then becomes a vicious cycle for empaths. You can avoid this trap by eating foods that are connected to the earth such as brothy soups and root vegetables. Additionally, eat a lot of good whole-grain carbohydrates.

Get Enough Sleep: Sleep is important because it is during this time that the body rejuvenates and repairs itself. When you don't get enough sleep, you feel tired and irritated, which can cause overwhelm for an empath. Empaths can find it difficult to sleep because of their highly sensitive nature, but there are things you can do to get a better night's sleep such as drinking a cup of chamomile tea an hour before going to bed. Stop looking at screens including your phone, TV, and laptop an hour before going to bed. Take a bath to relax the body and wear a sleep mask to block out any light.

Eliminate Stimulants: Coffee is considered a stimulant because it contains caffeine. Alcohol is also a stimulant because it alters your state of mind. Since empaths are naturally sensitive, consuming stimulants can send you into overdrive. Try a non-stimulant challenge for 30 days. It will help you tune into your gift even further because you are in your natural state and can focus on reality instead of taking on each day in an altered state.

Meditation: Science proves that meditation is a powerful grounding technique. The problem is that not many people know how to meditate properly, and nor do they understand the purpose of the practice. The main aim of meditation is not to provide some magical solution to clear your mind and get into a Zen-like state. The goal is to clear the mind of mental disturbance to increase awareness so that you connect with who you truly are and not with your thoughts. However, there is a misconception that to meditate effectively, one must empty the mind and think of nothing. This is one of the many reasons why people find it so difficult. You are always going to have thoughts, it's what makes you human. During meditation, the idea is to get you to focus on one idea instead of the many worries and frustrations of life that typically run through the mind. There is a lot more to meditation than this, but that's yet another book I could write. Getting into a daily habit of mediation will help you become grounded so you can cope more effectively with the challenges that come with being an empath. Here are some instructions for beginners taken from the mindful.org website:

- Get into a comfortable sitting position and start taking slow, deep breaths.
- Focus on your breath and pay attention to where it's coming from the most. Is it your nose or your stomach? Keep your focus on your inhale and exhale.
- Keep taking slow, deep breaths, and keep your focus on your breath for two minutes.

And that's it. When you feel your mind wandering, bring it back to your breath. Start by meditating for two minutes per day; as you start getting better at it, you can increase the time.

Epsom Salt Bath: Epsom salt comes from the earth and the earth is where empaths feel most connected. There are many advantages to Epsom salt, and one of them is its ability to cleanse an environment of negative energy. When you are surrounded by negative people, or when you get stuck in a cycle of negative thinking, the negative energy gets stuck in your energy field and this is what causes that drained and depressed feeling that empaths are so prone to. Due to its powerful cleansing ability, Epsom salt baths are a powerful tool to help empaths remain grounded. They eliminate all clogged negative energy and toxic vibrations. You can also add some crystals and essential oils to the bath to further clear and balance your energy field. In general, here are some of the main benefits of an Epsom salt bath:

- Improves the nervous system
- Glowing skin
- Eliminates constipation
- Relieves muscle cramps and pain
- Better sleep
- Soothes migraine headaches
- Relaxes the mind and body

Here are some steps for how to have an Epsom salt bath:

- Add two heaped cups of Epsom salt to the bath.
- Fill the bath with hot water and stir to dissolve the salt.
- Soak in the bath for at least 15 minutes.
- After soaking, rinse off in the shower to remove the salt from your body.

You can add to the experience by playing relaxing music and dimming the lights.

Earthing Sandals: Empaths have deep love and compassion for Mother Earth, but many empaths find it difficult to ground themselves. It isn't something they instinctively know how to do; grounding is a skill they've got to learn. Let me explain a little bit furthe … the physical body is made from all the components of Mother Earth, therefore, I would be justified in saying that we are all children of the earth. When we are surrounded by nature, we emit the same frequency as the earth, and this is what gives us life. This frequency provides healing and gives us everything we need to live an abundant life.

Many thousands of years ago, our ancestors walked around barefooted, but I can only assume that after one too many feet cut up on rocky ground, they came up with the ingenious idea to cover their feet with shoes. According to historians, the earliest footwear was earthing sandals. This enabled people to walk comfortably without worrying about the things on the ground that might harm them. As a result of wearing shoes, walking shorter distances, and carrying less, the shape of our feet changed; they became narrower, and tight-fitting shoes started causing bunions. Basically, wearing shoes separated us from the grounding energies of the earth.

Over time, harder materials have been used to make the soles of shoes. When our ancestors first started wearing shoes, they were made from all-natural materials. But today, we need to protect our feet for so many other reasons that shoes are made from materials so strong that we have no connection with the earth when we wear them. Wearing earthing sandals is a great idea if you are prepared to make them yourself because unfortunately, you won't find a company that makes them out of 100% compostable and sustainable materials. Therefore, your only alternative is to make your own; if you are up for the challenge, here is a great website to assist you.

A Moon Bath: For thousands of years, it has been believed that the moon has a powerful effect on women. Many women believe the moon influences their moods. Some have reported that they are more sensitive, and their emotions are heightened during the new and full moon. Additionally, experts state the best time to start a new project is during a full moon. In Ayurveda, a traditional form of Indian medicine, they use the moon to reduce heat in the body. But it is also used to balance energy, because the moon emits yin energy, and this helps balance the yang energy that comes from direct sun rays. According to author Nadine Artemis, lunar energy from the moon helps promote wellness and healing in the body. To benefit from it, you will need to familiarize yourself with the different moon cycles. Artemis recommends going outside when the moon is in its waning gibbous, waxing gibbous, and full moon phases. Basically, the best time for moon bathing is when the moon is at its brightest.

If you are not familiar with this practice, you are probably wondering how you take a moon bath. There are a couple of ways you can do this: you can either go outside during a full moon and take part in a ceremony that involves smearing frankincense under the nostrils and the brow, relaxing and taking deep breaths under the stars. Apparently, doing it naked and sleeping under the moon provides the most benefits, but that is entirely up to you.

Another way to take a moon bath is to fill some jars up with spring water and leave them outside after the sun has set. Collect the jars just before the sun comes up and pour the water into the bath. When you bring the jars inside, make sure they don't touch the ground before pouring the water into the bath.

The simplest way, however, is to soak in a bath when there is a full moon; this would be a good time to have an Epsom salt bath. Ensure that all artificial lights are switched off, and instead, use candles. Before getting into the bath, make a cup of lemon or rose tea, as they are packed with antioxidants and provide an extra dose of hydration. Soak in the bath for 30 minutes while taking deep breaths.

Practice Tai Chi: Tai Chi is a form of Chinese martial arts that emphasizes stability and lower body strength. The movements help you become conscious of the present moment due to the harmonious nature in which the mind and body work together when one is practicing Tai Chi. It repairs the body's nervous system and promotes a calmer state of mind. It is especially beneficial for empaths because it centers the body and helps them connect to the earth as well as helping to regulate the flow of energy.

To reap the full benefits of Tai Chi, you will need to learn with a qualified and experienced Master. If you don't have the budget for this, there are some basic moves you can practice alone. The good news is that there are plenty of YouTube videos you can watch for detailed instructions; but first, you will need to warm up. Below are a few exercises to get the blood flowing.

TAI CHI WARM-UP EXERCISES

- **Simple stretch:** Lean forward with your arms outstretched and touch your toes. Put your hands on your hips and come back up slowly.
- **Head rolls:** Take deep breaths while gently rolling your head in a circle from one side to another.
- **Picking fruit:** Stand with your feet shoulder-width apart and reach upward.
- **Knee circles:** Stand with your feet together, place your hands on your knees, bend your knees slightly, and then move them around in a circle.
- **Hip rolls:** Put your hands on your hips and stand with your feet shoulder-width apart. Roll your hips from one side to the other by pretending as if you are hula-hooping.
- **Shoulder rolls:** Stretch your arms out to the sides and move your arms in a circular motion.

Massage: Massage is an effective way to release stuck negative energy. The muscles in the body become tight because they are holding on to negative emotions. These tight areas are kneaded out during a massage and the negative energy is released. If going to see a massage therapist is not in your budget, you can give yourself a perfectly good massage in the comfort of your own home. Here are some instructions taken from the backintelligence website:

TIPS FOR SELF-MASSAGING

- You don't need to spend more than 2 minutes giving yourself a massage for it to be effective.
- Give yourself a massage twice a day for the best results.
- Run your fingers over your muscles until you locate the pain before you start applying pressure.
- Apply firm pressure, but start light and work your way up; you will know your tolerance level.
- If you find that the area is more painful after the massage, you probably applied too much pressure, so be more gentle next time.
- After your treatment, stretch out the area.

SELF-MASSAGE FOR THE HEAD

- Position your thumbs in front of your eardrums.
- Rest your fingertips on your temples.
- Use your fingertips to apply gentle pressure to your temples, moving in a circular motion.
- Travel along your hairline and keep making circular motions. Your fingertips will meet in the middle.

Self-Massage For the Neck

- Position three fingertips where your shoulders meet your neck.
- Hold onto the area and apply firm pressure.
- When you start feeling the muscles relax, release the hold.
- Slowly roll your shoulders forward and backward.

Self-Massage For the Shoulders

- Place the fingers of your right hand over your right shoulder. You will feel the dip in the muscle that connects your shoulder to your neck.
- Squeeze the muscle three times and then starting from the outside, roll your fingers over the muscle and upwards towards the base of your neck.
- Do the same with the left shoulder.

Self-Massage For the Lower Back

- You will need a tennis ball or a massage ball.
- Lean against a wall and then put the ball between your lower back and the wall.
- Move your body until you find the area of tension.
- Once you have found the tension, apply stronger pressure until you find a release.

SELF-MASSAGE FOR THE CHEST

- You will need a Thera Cane.
- Position the hook of the Thera Cane underneath your collarbone.
- Release the trigger point by applying downward pressure.
- Work the whole muscle by moving the hook so you can apply pressure at different angles.
- Repeat on the other side.

SELF-MASSAGE FOR THE LEGS

- You will need a foam roller.
- Lie on your side and place your hip on top of the foam roller.
- Balance yourself with your hands and roll downwards towards your knee. As you move, twist your body towards the ground.
- Roll back so the foam roller is under your hip again.
- Do the same on the other leg.

SELF-MASSAGE FOR THE FEET

- You will need a tennis ball or a massage ball.
- Take your shoes and socks off and sit on a chair.
- Place the tennis ball under your foot.
- Apply firm pressure and roll your foot back and forward from toe to heel over the ball.

- When you hit a tender spot, roll your foot in small circles to get the knot out.
- Do the same on the other foot.
- You can do this standing up if you want to add additional pressure.

SELF-MASSAGE FOR THE HIPS AND BUTTOCKS

- You will need a tennis ball or a massage ball.
- Place the tennis ball under one buttock, position your hands on the ground behind your back to steady yourself.
- Lift the other leg up and roll on the ball in small circles. When you find a tender area, roll on it more.
- Do the same on the other buttock.

SELF-MASSAGE FOR THE HANDS

- Hold onto your wrist in the same way you would take your pulse.
- Across your wrist, apply side-to-side pressure.
- Apply pressure to the heel of your palms and move your fingers in a circular motion, work your way around your hand.
- Grab hold of the area between your thumb and forefinger and massage it in a circular motion.
- Massage each finger in a circular motion moving upwards.
- When you get to the fingertip, pull the finger upwards.

Note: Ground yourself daily, don't wait until you feel over-whelmed. By making grounding a daily habit, you will in-crease in focus and you will always be prepared for the challenges life can throw at you.

CHAPTER 15:

HOW TO TURN YOUR EMPATH GIFT INTO A SUPERPOWER

Your empath ability is a superpower. I love watching superhero movies because I like to see how superheroes use their superpowers. Some superpowers you can learn through extensive training, but others you are born with. Empaths are born with their gift and this is what makes them unique; no one can learn how to be an empath. But in superhero movies, no one starts operating

in the full strength of their gift right away; they've got to go through a period of training to perfect it. For example, the great martial arts expert Shang-Chi is an extraordinary hand-to-hand fighter. There are not many that can compare to him in the Marvel Universe. He trained Spider Man and helped him develop a technique called Spider-Fu. Domino's luck power was more passive until she started training with Shang-Chi and developed it further. So what am I saying? Don't feel discouraged if you feel that your empath gift is more of a burden than a blessing. It's only because you haven't developed it fully and turned it into your superpower yet. Some empaths are lucky enough to have been raised with empath parents who passed on their gift to their children and trained them in it. If you are not one of those people, you might want to consider looking for a mentor like Shang-Chi to train you. But the reality is that mentors are difficult to come by, so you can train yourself to become the powerful empath warrior you were created to be. Here are some tips to get you started:

Trust Your Intuition: People either live in their heads and make decisions based on logic, or they are guided by their intuition and seem to get it right every time. Intuition, also referred to as "your gut feeling," is an inborn ability to acquire knowledge about a particular situation without conscious effort and reasoning. When you ignore your gut feeling and do the wrong thing, it's only when you are faced with the same consequences that you will recall you had a bad feeling about it before going ahead. The good news is that you can avoid this outcome by practicing these steps:

- **Get Still:** I refer to intuition as a voiceless voice, and to listen to it, you must be in a place of calm. With the hectic world we live in, and the one hundred and one things we have in our environments fighting for our attention, this is not an easy task. Therefore, you will need to set aside time to relax and get still. I would advise that you make this a part of your morning routine. Some empaths report that mediation works well for them. You can learn how to meditate in chapter 5.

- **Practice Mindfulness:** Mindfulness trains you to become more attentive to the things that are taking place within your external and internal environment. As mentioned, meditation helps you become still by quieting the mind. But mindfulness techniques will help you tune in to yourself and the world through making a conscious effort to focus and notice things. Again, practice makes perfect, so incorporate mindfulness into your daily routine. Experts suggest that ten minutes a day will make a significant difference. Since empaths are such emotional people, the "naming your emotions" mindfulness technique is a good place to start because it will help you determine what you are feeling, especially when the emotion doesn't come from you:

- When you feel an emotion, close your eyes and focus on it.
- Without passing judgment, give the emotion a name.
- Often, we confuse our emotions, and feeling upset is not the same as being frustrated, sad, or angry.

- **Give It a Try:** Sometimes, just thinking about something isn't enough, and you won't know whether something is good for you unless you give it a try. For example, let's say you are thinking about becoming a professional gardener because you like plants. Go ahead and take a Garden Design course because you might find that, even though you like plants, you don't enjoy working outside in the cold, or on the hard landscaping tasks that come with it. If you need to make a decision and are not sure what to do, give it a try and see how you feel.

- **Use Your Body as a Pendulum:** You may have heard of using a crystal or a pendulum on a chain as a dowsing tool to look for lost objects, or to gather the information we need. However, using our bodies as the pendulum or crystal is much more effective because it puts us in tune with our inner being. Using your body as a pendulum involves asking your higher self a question, and then waiting for your body to tilt in a forward or a backward motion. The first step is to determine how your higher self communicates with you by centering your body and asking yourself the direction for, "Yes," and "No," and then paying attention to the direction that your body moves. Your body will either tilt forwards for "yes" or backward for "no." Using your body as a pendulum takes a while to master so you will need a lot of practice to get it right.

- **Use Wisdom Cards:** When you are not sure about something or someone, use wisdom cards. They are also known as power animal cards and energy cards. Some people also use color cards, image cards, idea cards, or goddess cards. Use whatever card set feels right for you. There are several ways to consult cards, but the simplest way is to shuffle the card set and think of the confusion, doubt, or question you want clarity on. Position the cards so they are facing downwards and allow your hand to move over the cards. Your hand will naturally want to stop somewhere; chose a card, and reflect on what it says or shows. You can either take the meaning on the card literally, or as a metaphor, a symbol, an image, or a story related to the question you've asked.

- **Pay Attention to Synchronicities:** Jungian psychology and esoteric wisdom has long held that every coincidence carries a meaning and provides guidance as they correspond to our inner experiences and emotional states. Some people refer to them as nods and winks from the universe letting us know, if we pay attention, that we are on the right track. You might have days when you see the same sequence of numbers such as 22:22, 44:44, or 11:11 in different locations that have no relation to the other. You might run into the same person (whether you know them or not) three times in the same week. You might go through a period when everything seems to point in the direction of a certain city. We all have coincidences in our lives, but most of us don't pay attention to them. Once you start paying attention to synchronicities, you will find it easier to tune into your gut feeling because the signs will confirm how you are feeling.

- **Make a Commitment:** Your inner wisdom is more powerful than you can imagine. It will always guide you in the right direction if you listen. After practicing the above techniques, decide that you are no longer going to question your intuition, trust that it is right every time and follow it. You can start by using your intuition to guide you with the decisions that are not so important, and then work your way up. Don't worry if you're not right all the time, the idea is to get familiar with the feeling when you are right, then you will always know when something is wrong.

How to Improve Your Psychic Ability: Unless you were raised in a household where highly sensitive traits were the norm, there is a good chance you were encouraged to suppress your psychic abilities. In general, adults don't take children seriously, but see them as tiny beings who don't have any experience in the world. A sensitive child is often told to stop being silly. Seeing ghosts is considered a figment of their imagination and talking to Grandpa who died before you were born is definitely impossible. However, the reality is that in general, children are very in tune with the spiritual world because they are more sensitive. In most cases, their world is perfect, full of clouds and rainbows. As a result, children feel more, hear more, and see more. The creator gave us these survival instincts to help us safely move through the world. Through the conditioning we receive as children, we start to believe that intuition and emotions have no real importance in a world where most people are struggling to pay bills and survive. So we turn our noses up at mediums, clairvoyants, and anyone else who has psychic abilities, and accept that the most important aspect of our reality is the physical world. But not to worry cosmic warriors, with a bit of practice you can fully revive your psychic abilities. The first step is to get in touch with your intuition, which has already been discussed above.

- **Scan Your Environment:** Practicing environmental scans is a great way to cultivate your psychic abilities. To do this, move into the center of a room. From here, you can either move around the area or scan it with your eyes and pay attention to the scents, sounds, and sights. Which areas do you find most appealing? Which areas do you find the least appealing? Explore everything; the furniture, the windows, and the corners. How does the energy coming from these places make you feel? You will find this exercise a bit strange to begin with, especially if you are in a room with other people, just do it discreetly, and no one will notice what's going on. Practice environmental scans in cars, subways, parks, offices, and bars. Anywhere you go, perform an environmental scan. The idea is to train yourself to become aware of your surroundings so you can quickly tune into the subtle shifts in energy. Eventually, you will be able to use this skill to access memories and future events.

- **Access Your Subconscious Mind:** It is normal to protect ourselves from information overload. There is so much going on in the world that we can't afford to absorb everything, so whether consciously or unconsciously, we create boundaries to protect ourselves. Nevertheless, the most effective way of tapping into your psychic ability is through the subconscious mind, and one way to access it is through dreams. When we are free from psychological constraints we can effortlessly move between spaces. Dreams are a gateway to the unseen world, and the more familiar we become with the subconscious world, the more in tune we become with our psychic powers. You can connect with your dreams by keeping a pen and paper by your bed, and as soon as you awake from a dream, write it down. You will soon start to realize how connected the physical and the spiritual world really are.

- **Tune Into Energy:** When empaths get bad vibes from people, they tune out because they can sometimes live in a fantasy world where everyone is good, and when that fantasy is interrupted with negative vibes, it's disturbing for them. But tuning in to a person's negative energy can help strengthen your skills. Delve deeper into the energy of the new people you meet by looking beyond how they speak and the way they look. Instead, get your information about them by tuning into their energy. You might be asking, "Well, how is this possible?" When you are in the person's presence, pay attention to their energy and see what you pick up. Start a conversation with them on the topic of what you can sense and see whether your instincts were correct.

How to Improve Your Healing Ability: Some empaths have a healing gift; they instinctively know when a person has an ailment in the body. But what some empaths are not aware of is that they also have the power to heal that ailment by rebalancing their energy. This type of healing is common in Asian and African cultures, but it is dismissed in the Western world because we are only focused on the physical healing of the body. As far as Western medicine is concerned, once the symptoms have been treated, the person is cured. But what we fail to understand is that unless the root cause is treated, full healing will never manifest. In fact, it is not uncommon for ailments to return shortly after taking a course of medicine to get rid of them. Healing is a powerful gift because it is life-giving. But as with all gifts, it must be perfected, or it can cause more harm than good. Here are some tips on how to improve your healing ability:

- **Raise Your Vibrations:** Energy is not static; it moves, and that movement is vibration. When the body is not vibrating at its optimal frequency, an imbalance occurs and can cause physical ailments. Therefore, your first step as a healer is to learn how to sense vibrations:

  - Rub your hands together in a firm motion for 30 seconds to one minute.
  - With your palms facing each other, cup your hands and slowly pull them apart. The tingling feeling you notice is the vibration.
  - Keep pulling your hands apart until the tingling feeling goes away.
  - Slowly move your hands back towards each other, paying attention to when the tingling feeling starts again.
  - Vibration is also sensed through sound. Hum for 30 seconds while closing your eyes.
  - Pay attention to where and how you feel the vibration in your body.

- **Entertainment:** In energy healing, the use of an object such as a crystal, essential oil, or a singing bowl is referred to as using "entertainment" to bring our vibration into alignment with the object. Entertainment is how energy healing works; when two objects vibrating at different frequencies are placed next to each other, they lock into phase, and one vibrates higher while the other vibrates lower.

- **Your Mindset:** If you are not in the right state of mind, healing through energy balance is impossible. You will need the following to facilitate healing effectively:

  - **Discipline:** To improve your healing skills, you will need to practice them daily for no less than 10 weeks. The main aim is to ensure that your ability to heal becomes a normal part of your life.

  - **Positive Emotions:** Positive emotions carry high vibrations; negative emotions carry low vibrations. So, you will need to make a conscious effort to make joy, gratitude, and peace a daily habit.

  - **Focus:** A distracted mind can't heal; you must be able to focus intensely on the task at hand to get the best results.

  - **Flexibility:** Healing is not a straightforward process, and during a healing session, you might find that a person has many emotional blockages that are preventing them from experiencing full healing. You will need to be able to sense those blockages and clear them before getting back to the original intention.

- **The Power of Intention:** Intention is an essential tool for healing because if you believe it, you can achieve it. Studies prove the power of intention; sick people have been healed after taking a placebo sugar pill. In other words, the patients believed the sugar pill would heal them, and it did. So when you set out with the intention of healing, you will achieve it. Intention is more than a set goal, it is directed energy, and when the intention of healing is directed towards the body, healing will manifest. To become an effective healer, you will need to intensify your intention. Here are some tips to help you:

    - **Clear Blockages:** When a sink is blocked, the first thing we do is look for a plunger to unblock it because we want the water to flow freely. If you have blockages in your energy field, you are going to find it difficult to set strong enough intentions that enable healing to manifest. Blockages are often related to fear and self-limiting beliefs. Do some soul searching and find out what they are; you clear the blockage by confronting it. If it is more deeply rooted and you need counseling to overcome it, go ahead and do that. But either way, you must make a decision that you are going to overcome these blockages so you can become the powerful healer you were created to be.

- **Develop a Healthy Relationship:** As mentioned, energy healing is frowned upon in the Western world. But that's only because it's misunderstood. As a result, some empaths are made to feel as if their gift is not valid, or that it's spooky or scary in some way. Out of fear of being judged, they shy away from their gift and this can harm their ability to set strong intentions. If this sounds like you, it's time to develop a healthy relationship with your gift and accept that it's wonderful and powerful, and that once it's perfected, it will help a lot of people.

- **Improve Your Focus:** The stronger your ability to focus, the more powerful your intentions will become. As mentioned, intention is setting your energy towards a particular outcome, and a strong focus will intensify the intention. One of the ways to improve your focus is through meditation. You can read more about meditation in chapter 5.

Free Yourself from the Victim Mentality: Being an empath is not a negative attribute, but when people don't understand their gift, it's easy for them to get caught up in the victim mentality. Carrying the weight of the world on your shoulders is definitely a burden, there is no doubt about that. But when you know how to carry that weight, it becomes a blessing. Empaths are prone to sickness and depression because they don't know how to protect themselves from the negative energy that keeps getting trapped in their system. Here are some tips on how to free yourself from the victim mentality:

- **Stop Blaming People:** As you have read, empaths are people pleasers. They will go to the ends of the earth to ensure everyone around them is happy. All of this is done with a smile on their faces, but there is a continuous negative dialogue taking place on the inside saying things like, "I really don't have time for this," "Can't she tell how much this is stressing me out?" or "If my mother wasn't such a negative person, I wouldn't feel this way all the time." Thoughts of this nature are disastrous for your mental health, and the end result is bitterness and frustration. Becoming assertive and learning how to protect your energy are all parts of the process. A lot of what empaths feel is self-inflicted; think about it: if you know that traveling twenty miles outside of your area during rush hour traffic will mean you get home too late to complete your assignment, meaning you will have to stay up all night so you don't miss your deadline, whose fault is it if you say "yes?" When you are fully aware of the inconvenience that comes with saying "yes," you only have yourself to blame when you are left to deal with the consequences of your actions.

Once you understand that you can protect your power by not giving it away, you will stop blaming people because you won't have anyone to blame.

- **Be Kind to Yourself:** Do you struggle to love yourself because of low-self-esteem or a past moral failure? If you suffer from low self-esteem, what are the things that you don't like about yourself? Are you overweight? Do you hate your job? There are many things in our life that we have full control over and can change if we decide that we want to. It is your responsibility to take action and go after the things you want. If you have done something you regret, remember that you are not the first person to make a mistake and you won't be the last. The key is to learn from that mistake and move forward, not dwell on it. If there is one thing we can't do, it's go back in time to change the past, but we can control the future, so that should be your main focus.

- **Practice Gratitude:** You might not be where you want to be, but there are plenty of things in your life you can be grateful for right now. Gratitude puts you in the right frame of mind because it takes your focus off the negative and sets it on the positive. You can read more about gratitude in chapter 3.

- **Stop Self-Sabotaging:** What are the things you are doing that are hindering your progress? People who see themselves as victims don't believe they are worthy of good things. As a result, they will unconsciously do things to self-sabotage. For example, if they know they've got an exam coming up, the self-sabotager won't study because deep down, they don't feel deserving of getting the qualifications they need that will secure them their dream job. Instead, they will procrastinate and cram at the last minute. When they fail, the victim mentality kicks in, because an F confirms how they feel deep down – like a failure. They ignore the fact that they contributed to that failure.

- **Find the Root of the Problem:** Some empaths soar like eagles while others flap around in their chicken coop trying to make it. Why is this? Because the successful empaths refuse to allow their past to hinder their future. Did you have a bad childhood? Did you get involved in an abusive relationship? Have you suffered from some type of trauma? Whatever it is, find out the root of your problems – and you may need to get professional help for this. But once you find out the root, determine that you are not going to allow it to stop you from becoming who you were created to be.

Transmute Negative Energy

As an empath, you will have walked into a room and sensed the hostility and negative energy of other people. Or you are upset with someone, and you are talking to them with a smile on your face, but deep down you are seething with anger. I don't need to tell you that the spiritual world is more important than the physical world because empaths operate on a deep spiritual level. The invisible dimension that no one else can see is who we really are. But we live in a culture that doesn't acknowledge this, and instead the focus is on the things we can see. But at the same time, we are constantly emitting energy, whether positive or negative, into our environment. You can compare negative energy to a poisonous arrow that affects our entire physical system. This energy is transmitted through our thoughts and feelings and it has a powerful influence on our environment.

There is not one person on the planet who doesn't experience negative feelings, it's human nature. Anger, fear, frustration, and sadness are all emotions that make us who we are. The problem isn't that we have these emotions, it's that we store them in our subconscious mind, and they become a stumbling block for ourselves and others. Additionally, you need to know the type of interactions and situations that trigger you, and then learn to express those thoughts and feelings in a healthy way. In doing so, we learn how to transmute negative energy into positive energy.

Spirituality teaches us that what is taking place in our outer world is a reflection of what's going on inside. But regardless of the negative energy that comes your way, you have the power to transform it into something positive. Here are some tips on how to do so:

- **Breathe:** Negative emotions cause shallow breathing; however, deep breathing transforms the reactive state and relaxes you.

- **Set Your Intention:** When you get angry or upset, take a few deep breaths and then repeat the following statement: "I am feeling [name the emotion] and I need to express how I feel. I am commanding the energy of my feelings to transform into light and love, so I am flooding my environment with positive energy."

- **Think of Something Important to You:** What are you passionate about? Maybe it's an animal such as a cat or a dog. Maybe you have a child or a friend who is totally in tune with you. When you start feeling negative energy, think of what's important to you and connect with the positive emotions you experience.

- **Use Your Words:** I have always believed that the most powerful weapon in the world is the tongue. We can speak life, or we can speak death with it; it's easy to get into the habit of speaking negatively, especially when that's how you feel. However, you can make a conscious decision to fill your mouth with words that are pure, loving, and kind instead of verbalizing negative energy.

- **Don't Pity People:** Instead of feeling sorry for people who are in difficult situations, empower them with the strength they need to get out of it. Empaths are good at pitying people because they feel what they feel. But this is not how to encourage someone. In fact, demonstrating pity gives them an incentive to remain in their condition. Instead, assist them in finding the solutions to their problems, and if you can, help them reach the resolution.

You are more powerful than you can imagine, you can choose to conquer your inaction by taking massive action. Your empath gift could have been given to someone else, but it was given to you; therefore, don't allow yourself to simply go with the flow of your circumstances, thoughts, and feelings. Don't trade in your superpower for something less meaningful. Become focused, clear, and concise about making important decisions in the moment that are not dictated by external factors. If you are going to become extraordinary, choice is the only thing that matters... CHOOSE TO BE GREAT!

CONCLUSION

Empaths are emotional sponges, so when there's an emotion, they absorb it, and because of this, they can sometimes suppress how they truly feel. You are prone to neglecting yourself because you don't feel comfortable going to others with your problems. The irony is that the more you bottle things up, the more your energy is depleted and there is less of you to give to others – and helping people is what you want more than anything else in the world. Nevertheless, once you have mastered the art of detaching yourself from others, you will find it easier to take care of yourself. The first step to achieving this is being fully connected to your inner soul so that you can hear the cry of your heart and articulate it in a way that everyone can understand. Remember, the majority of people are not empaths, and they won't be able to feel what you feel, so unless you spell it out to them, they will never know.

The universe is interconnected, we are all one, and empaths can feel this deeply. However, even though we are all connected, you should always remain your first priority; if not, you'll become overwhelmed, frustrated, and disillusioned with life. Therefore, only offer a helping hand when it's not going to inconvenience you significantly. You can only give what you have; anything more will cause you to become imbalanced, which then becomes counterproductive because operating in the fullness of your empath gift requires balance in all areas of your life.

You are capable of giving more than the average person. But how you choose to use your gift is your own personal decision. My prayer is that you will use it for the greater good in this world, first by becoming all you were destined to be, and then applying it for the benefit of humanity.

May your journey to enhance your empath gift be filled with courage, joy, and fulfillment of purpose... be blessed!

THANKS FOR READING!

I really hope you enjoyed this book, and most of all, got more value from it than you had to give.

It would mean a lot to me if you left an Amazon review – I will reply to all questions asked!

Simply find this book on Amazon, scroll to the reviews section, and click "Write a customer review".

Or alternatively please visit www.pristinepublish.com/empathreview to leave a review

Be sure to check out my email list, where I am constantly adding tons of value.

The best way to get on it currently is by visiting www.pristinepublish.com/hygge/ and entering your email.

Here I'll provide actionable information that aims to improve your enjoyment of life.

I'll update you on my latest books and I'll even send free e-books that I think you'll find useful.

Kindest regards,

TAKE YOUR EMPATH GIFT TO THE NEXT LEVEL

There is so much to the empath gift that it's impossible to fit it all into one book. So, based on some of the most popular requests, I decided to put together a second book called *The Empowered Empath*. And boy were there some interesting finds! I didn't want to stop writing, and who knows, there might be a part three.

My life soared once I began to apply the principles I learned through taking advice from mature empaths who are walking in the fullness of their calling, and reading books on being highly sensitive. The knowledge available is profound, and once I tapped into it, I literally experienced a supernatural transformation. However, what I found on my journey was that I often got overwhelmed by the massive amount of information I was exposed to. This is one of the reasons why I decided to start writing books to help other empaths. I wanted to condense what I have learned to make it easier for empaths and highly sensitive people to digest.

In my second book, *The Empowered Empath*, I delve much deeper into the spiritual side of being an empath. In it, you will gain further insight into the following topics:

- **Understanding energy:** Discover the limitless mind-blowing possibilities you can tap into once you understand how energy works.

- **How to become an assertive empath:** Learn how to articulate what you need so that people won't be able to take advantage of you.

- **How to set boundaries:** Uncover the powerful freedom available to you when you know how to set boundaries and stick to them.

- **How to control your emotions:** Find out how to process your emotions and how to stop allowing them to overwhelm you.

- **How to find peace living in a cruel world:** Master focusing on the positive around you instead of the negative.

Get ready to take your empath gift to the next level and enter into new realms of power!

Visit: www.pristinepublish.com/judybooks

ALSO BY
Judy Dyer

Grasp a better understanding of your gift and how you can embrace every part of it so your life is enriched day by day.

Visit: www.pristinepublish.com/judybooks

ESSENTIAL OIL RECIPES FOR ANXIETY

QUICK AND EASY LAVENDER NECK RUB

Ingredients

- 3 drops of pure lavender
- 1 teaspoon of fractioned almond or coconut oil

Directions

Combine the lavender oil and almond or coconut oil in the palms of your hands and rub directly onto your neck. You can also rub the mixture onto the soles of your feet; this is particularly effective before bedtime.

Men's Cologne

Ingredients

- 5 drops of cedarwood essential oil
- 3 drops of bergamot essential oil
- 2 drops of sandalwood essential oil
- 8 ounces of 70 percent alcohol
- Glass cologne tube or glass roll-on tube

Directions

Combine all the ingredients in the cologne tube or glass roll, shake together thoroughly and use whenever required.

FRANKINCENSE AND MYRRH LOTION

This homemade body lotion made from a mixture of frankincense and myrrh is a fantastic recipe. Not only does it alleviate anxiety symptoms, but it also hydrates the skin with essential nutrients and vitamins.

Ingredients

- ¼ cup of olive oil
- ¼ cup of coconut oil
- ¼ cup of beeswax
- ¼ cup of shea butter
- 2 tablespoons of vitamin E
- 20 drops of frankincense essential oil
- 20 drops of myrrh essential oil
- Plastic lotion dispenser bottles

Directions

1. Combine shea butter, beeswax, coconut oil, and olive oil in a bowl.

2. Add some water to a large saucepan and heat over a medium temperature until it starts to boil. Place the bowl into the saucepan and heat the ingredients, while stirring the mixture.

3. Remove the bowl from the stove and place it in the fridge for an hour or until it becomes solid.

4. Remove the mixture from the fridge and use an electric hand mixer to whisk the ingredients until fluffy. Combine the vitamin E and the essential oils and continue to mix.

5. Add to the plastic lotion dispenser bottles and store in a cool place.

HOMEMADE LAVENDER SOAP BAR

This homemade bar of lavender soap not only provides relief from anxiety but is also extremely beneficial for the skin. It's simple to make, free from chemicals, and easy on the wallet.

Ingredients

- 20-30 drops of lavender essential oil
- Soap base
- 3 drops of vitamin E
- Decorative soap mold or oval bar molds

Directions

1. Add water to a large pan and heat it over a medium temperature until it starts to boil.

2. Add the soap base to a glass bowl and then place the bowl in the saucepan until the base has melted.

3. Take the bowl out of the saucepan and allow it to cool down. Add the vitamin E and the lavender and stir together thoroughly.

4. Transfer the mixture to a soap mold. Allow it to cool down and become completely solid before removing it from the soap mold. Store the soap at room temperature.

REFERENCES

Alcantara, M, *Chakra Healing: A Beginner's Guide to Self-Healing Techniques that Balance the Chakras* (Illustrated ed.), Althea Press, 2017.

Gray, K, *Raise Your Vibration: 111 Practices to Increase Your Spiritual Connection* (1st ed.), Hay House Inc, 2016.

Ma, N. M., *Getting Grounded Manual: A Manual of Grounding Exercises* (2nd ed.). Michael Nagel LLC, 2017.

Pittman, C. M., Mlis, K. E. M., Mars, S., & Wetware Media, *Rewire Your Anxious Brain: How to Use the Neuroscience of Fear to End Anxiety, Panic, and Worry*, Wetware Media, 2015.

Henderson, B, 2020, *Dr. Diane Malaspina: "How to Develop Mindfulness and Serenity During Stressful or Uncertain Times"*, Authority Magazine, viewed 18th Jan 2021 <https://medium.com/authority-magazine/dr-diane-malaspina-how-to-develop-mindfulness-and-serenity-during-stressful-or-uncertain-times-407b2d8c611d>

Whitbourne, S.K., 2020, *Is It Possible to Program Your Happiness?*, Psychology Today, viewed 18th Jan 2021

<https://www.psychologytoday.com/us/blog/fulfillment-any-age/202002/is-it-possible-program-your-happiness>

Tibi- Elhanany,Y & Shamay-Tsoory, S, 2011, *Social cognition in social anxiety: first evidence for increased empathic abilities*, PubMed, viewed 18th Jan 2021 <https://pubmed.ncbi.nlm.nih.gov/22120444/>

Seppala, E, Bradley, C & Goldstein, 2020, M.R., Research: *Why Breathing is So Effective at Reducing Stress*, Harvard Business Review, viewed 18th Jan 2021 <https://hbr.org/2020/09/research-why-breathing-is-so-effective-at-reducing-stress#:~:text=Research%20shows%20that%20different%20emotions,short%2C%20fast%2C%20and%20shallow.>

Centre for Clinical Interventions, 2008, *Module 4: How to Behave More Assertively,* viewed 18th Jan 2021 <https://cci.health.wa.gov.au/~/media/CCI/Consumer%20Modules/Assert%20Yourself/Assert%20Yourself%20-%2004%20-%20How%20to%20Behave%20More%20Assertively.pdf>

Animal Mind & Comms – Viikki, 2017, *Empathetic People Experience Dogs' Expressions More Strongly,* University of Helsinki, viewed 18th Jan 2021 <https://www.helsinki.fi/en/news/health/empathetic-people-experience-dogs-expressions-more-strongly>

Living Well, 2012, *Grounding Exercises,* viewed 18th Jan 2021 <https://www.livingwell.org.au/well-being/mental-health/grounding-exercises/>

Mindful Staff, 2019, *How to Meditate,* Mindful, viewed 18th Jan 2021 <https://www.mindful.org/how-to-meditate/>

Joa, 2019, *The 7 Easy Steps to Start Making Your Own Natural Grounding Shoes,* viewed 18th Jan 2021 <https://earthingmoccasins.com/diy-barefoot-sun-sandals/?v=11aedd0e4327>

Craig, J, 2017, *Can moon bathing soothe your body and mind?,* Moody Month, viewed 18th Jan 2021 <https://moodymonth.com/articles/can-moon-bathing-soothe-your-body-and-mind>

McQuilkie, S, 2020, *Self-Massage Techniques,* Back Intelligence, viewed 18th Jan 2021 <https://backintelligence.com/self-massage-techniques/>

Pinch, B, 2016, *More Than Just a Sugar Pill: Why the placebo effect is real,* Harvard University, viewed 18th Jan 2021 <http://sitn.hms.harvard.edu/flash/2016/just-sugar-pill-placebo-effect-real/>